The CURIOUS Book of LISTS

For Toby, Josh, Ollie, Sasha, Jasper,
Will, Maddy, and, of course,
Ades McGee.

A Raspberry Book
www.raspberrybooks.co.uk
Written by Tracey Turner
Illustrated by Caroline Selmes

Editorial: Kath Jewitt
Cover design: Sidonie Beresford-Browne
Design concept: Sidonie Beresford-Browne
Internal design: Sidonie Beresford-Browne and
Peter Clayman

KINGFISHER
LONDON & NEW YORK

Text and design copyright © Raspberry Books Ltd 2019
First published in 2019 in the United States by Kingfisher
This paperback edition published in 2022 by Kingfisher
120 Broadway, New York, NY 10271
Kingfisher is an imprint of Macmillan Children's Books, London
All rights reserved

Distributed in the United States and Canada by Macmillan,
120 Broadway, New York, NY 10271

EU representative: Macmillan Publishers Ireland Ltd, 1st Floor,
The Liffey Trust Centre, 117-126 Sheriff Street Upper, Dublin 1, D01 YC43

Library of Congress Cataloging-in-Publication data has been applied for.

ISBN 978-0-7534-7666-6

Kingfisher books are available for special promotions and premiums. For details contact:
Special Markets Department, Macmillan, 120 Broadway, New York, NY 10271.

For more information, please visit
www.kingfisherbooks.com

Printed in China
9 8 7 6 5 4 3 2 1
1TR/0322/WKT/UG/128MA

MIX
Paper from
responsible sources
FSC
www.fsc.org   FSC® C116313

The CURIOUS Book of LISTS

Tracey Turner AND Caroline Selmes

KINGFISHER
LONDON & NEW YORK

How to Say Hello in 9 Different LANGUAGES

1. **Spanish** Hola

2. **French** Bonjour

3. **Italian** Ciao

4. **Swahili** Jambo

5. **Portuguese** Olá

6. **Danish** God dag

8. **German** Guten tag

7. **Greek** Yasou

9. **Hebrew** Shalom

4 WHOPPING WHALES

- **BLUE WHALE**—up to 100 ft (30m) long, 200 tons (the biggest animal that's ever lived).
- **FIN WHALE**—up to 85 ft (26m) long, 88 tons.
- **SPERM WHALE**—up to 66 ft (20m) long, 55 tons (the biggest animal in the world with teeth, and the world's largest brain).
- **RIGHT WHALE**—up to 150 ft (46m), 72 tons.

7 Weirdly NAMED BODY Bits

1. **Zonule of Zinn, found in the eye.**
2. **Bachmann's bundle, found in the heart.**
3. **Space of Disse, found in the liver.**
4. Island of Reil, found in the brain.
5. **Islets of Langerhans, found in the pancreas.**
6. Loop of Henle, found in the kidney.
7. **Luschka's crypts, found in the gall bladder.**

37 Popular BREEDS OF DOGS

Australian shepherd • Basset hound • Beagle • Bernese mountain dog • Border collie • Boston terrier • Boxer • Bulldog • Cavalier King Charles spaniel • Cocker spaniel • Chihuahua • Dachshund • Doberman pinscher • French bulldog • German shepherd dog • German short-haired pointer • Golden retriever • Great Dane • Havanese • Labrador retriever • Maltese • Miniature schnauzer • Newfoundland • Pembroke Welsh corgi • Pomeranian • Poodle • Pug • Rhodesian ridgeback • Rottweiler • Shetland sheepdog • Shi tzu • Siberian husky • Springer spaniel • Vizsla • Weimaraner • West Highland terrier • Yorkshire terrier

8 Coral Reef FACTS

1. **Coral reefs only take up two percent of the sea floor, yet they are home to a quarter of all sea life.**

2. Coral reefs are made up of millions of tiny animals called corals, which are related to anemones and jellyfish. Hard corals build a chalky exoskeleton, which is how coral reefs are formed.

3. **It takes coral reefs a long time to form—most corals only grow less than 1 in (2.5cm) per year.**

4. The biggest coral reef in the world is the Great Barrier Reef off the coast of eastern Australia. It is about 1,400 mi (2,253km) long and is 20,000 years old.

5. Six of the world's seven species of sea turtles live on the Great Barrier Reef, which is also home to 400 species of coral, 1,500 species of fishes, and 4,000 species of mollusks.

6. Most coral reefs are in warm, shallow water, but not all of them. There are coral reefs all over the world, some in deep, cold water.

7. A change in water temperature can make coral turn white. Bleached coral is damaged, but can recover if the temperature of the water returns to normal quickly.

8. Around a quarter of the world's coral reefs are damaged too badly to regrow.

THE 7 WONDERS
OF THE ANCIENT WORLD

Only one of these Wonders survives today—the Great Pyramid at Giza.

THE LIGHTHOUSE AT ALEXANDRIA
The tallest building in the world when it was built, destroyed by an earthquake in the Middle Ages.

THE COLOSSUS OF RHODES
Giant bronze statue of the sun god Helios, destroyed by an earthquake around 200 BCE.

THE STATUE OF ZEUS AT OLYMPIA
Huge golden statue of the king of the Greek gods, destroyed by fire around 460 CE.

THE MAUSOLEUM AT HALICARNASSUS
Elaborate tomb for King Mausolus, destroyed by an earthquake in the Middle Ages.

THE GREAT PYRAMID AT GIZA
The 4,500-year-old massive stone tomb of Pharaoh Khufu still stands in Egypt.

THE HANGING GARDENS OF BABYLON
King Nebuchadnezzar's spectacular palace gardens, created more than 2,500 years ago.

THE TEMPLE OF ARTEMIS AT EPHESUS
Ancient Greek marble temple in honor of the goddess of hunting, destroyed by the Goths in 262 CE.

8
CURES FOR HICCUPS

No one knows why we get hiccups. Some of these cures are more useful than others, but there's no guarantee that any of them will work.

1. Think about pineapples.
2. Hold your breath.
3. Make yourself sneeze.
4. Sip ice-cold water.
5. Pull your tongue.
6. Bite a lemon.
7. Eat sugar.
8. Jump out of a plane (note: make sure you are wearing a parachute).

54 AFRICAN COUNTRIES

1. Algeria 2. Angola 3. Benin 4. Botswana 5. Burkina Faso 6. Burundi 7. Cabo Verde 8. Cameroon 9. Central African Republic 10. Chad 11. Comoros 12. Congo, Republic of the 13. Congo, Democratic Republic of the 14. Côte d'Ivoire 15. Djibouti 16. Egypt 17. Equatorial Guinea 18. Eritrea 19. Eswatini (formerly Swaziland) 20. Ethiopia 21. Gabon 22. Gambia 23. Ghana 24. Guinea 25. Guinea-Bissau 26. Kenya 27. Lesotho 28. Liberia 29. Libya 30. Madagascar 31. Malawi 32. Mali 33. Mauritania 34. Mauritius 35. Morocco 36. Mozambique 37. Namibia 38. Niger 39. Nigeria 40. Rwanda 41. Sao Tome and Principe 42. Senegal 43. Seychelles 44. Sierra Leone 45. Somalia 46. South Africa 47. South Sudan 48. Sudan 49. Tanzania 50. Togo 51. Tunisia 52. Uganda 53. Zambia 54. Zimbabwe

3 Really BIG SPIDERS

These are the three biggest spiders in the world. Although the giant huntsman is huge, it's not as heavy as either of the bird-eating spiders. By the way, bird-eating spiders really have been known to eat birds, but they usually feed on insects, small mammals, and frogs.

1. Goliath Bird-eating Spider
This spider has a 12-in (30-cm) leg span and fangs 1 in (2.5cm) long. Can deliver a nasty bite but not deadly to people.

2. Giant Huntsman Spider
This spider's leg span can be even bigger than the goliath bird-eating spider's, but it's much more spindly. Not dangerous to people.

3. Brazilian Salmon Pink Bird-eating Spider
Leg span up to 11 in (28cm). Can bite but not deadly to people.

5 ANCIENT OLYMPIC SPORTS

The first Olympic Games were held in Olympia, Greece, in 776 BCE. Only men could compete, although there was also a separate running race for unmarried women. Some of the sports were the same as in the modern Olympics. Two big differences were the sacrifice of 100 cows to the god Zeus, and the fact that the men competed naked.

1. **Pankration:** A bit like a cross between wrestling and boxing.

2. **Chariot Races:** Could be very dangerous, with charioteers jostling for position at high speeds.

3. **Boxing:** Unlike modern boxing, there were no weight categories.

4. **Hoplitodromos:** A running race wearing armor and carrying a shield.

5. **Wrestling:** Wrestlers were the most famous sports stars of Ancient Greece. Some were said to train by wrestling bulls.

12
Moon-walking Astronauts

Only twelve people have ever set foot on the Moon, and one of them, Alan Shepard, played golf on it.

NAME	SPACECRAFT	TIME ON THE MOON	MISSION DATES
Neil Armstrong	Apollo 11	2 hours 32 mins	July 16-24, 1969
Edwin "Buzz" Aldrin Jr.	Apollo 11	2 hours 15 mins	July 16-24, 1969
Charles Conrad Jr.	Apollo 12	7 hours 45 mins	November 14-24, 1969
Alan Bean	Apollo 12	7 hours 45 mins	November 14-24, 1969
Alan Shepard	Apollo 14	9 hours 23 mins	Jan 31-Feb 9, 1971
Edgar Mitchell	Apollo 14	9 hours 23 mins	Jan 31-Feb 9, 1971
David Scott	Apollo 15	19 hours 8 mins	July 26-August 7, 1971
James Irwin	Apollo 15	18 hours 35 mins	26 July-7 August 1971
John Young	Apollo 16	20 hours 14 mins	April 16-27, 1972
Charles Duke Jr.	Apollo 16	20 hours 14 mins	April 16-27, 1972
Eugene Cernan	Apollo 17	22 hours 4 mins	December 7-19, 1972
Harrison Schmitt	Apollo 17	22 hours 4 mins	December 7-19, 1972

Enormous
LAND ANIMALS

The weights given for these whopping great stompers are the maximum weight for each animal. The biggest African elephant weighs more than 100 average people.

1. **African elephant** (7.7 tons)
2. **White rhinoceros** (4.4 tons)
3. **Hippopotamus** (4.4 tons)
4. **Giraffe** (1.4 tons)
5. **Cape buffalo** (1.1 ton)
6. **American bison** (1.1 ton)
7. **Polar bear** (1,650 lb / 748kg)
8. **Tiger** (660 lb / 299kg)
9. **Gorilla** (485 lb / 220kg)

1.4 tons

7.7 tons

485 lb

4,4 tons

5 Slimy Animals

1. Hagfish
The eel-like hagfish feeds on dead sea creatures and produces lots of thick slime when attacked.

2. Violet Sea Snail
This snail floats on a raft of its own slime.

3. Velvet Worm
This animal shoots jets of slime up to 12 in (30cm) to trap its insect prey.

4. Parrotfish
The parrotfish covers itself in a thick layer of slime to sleep in.

5. Opossum
The opossum oozes green, foul-smelling slime from its rear end when threatened, and foams at the mouth at the same time.

8 WINNERS of THE MOST OLYMPIC MEDALS

1. **Michael Phelps (US, swimming):** 28
2. Larisa Latynina (Soviet Union, gymnastics): 18
3. **Nikolai Andrianov (Soviet Union, gymnastics):** 15
4. Marit Bjørgen (Norway, cross-country skiing): 15
5. **Boris Shakhlin (Soviet Union, gymnastics):** 13
6. Edoardo Mangiarotti (Italy, fencing): 13
7. **Takashi Ono (Japan, gymnastics):** 13
8. Ole Einar Bjørndalen (Norway, biathlon): 13

★ 3 Horrifying Creepy-Crawlies

1. **Camel spider**
Hairy, weird spider-lookalike with enormous jaws that can deliver a nasty bite.

2. **Japanese giant hornet**
The wasp of your worst nightmares, its sting can be fatal to people.

3. **House centipede**
Fast-moving, long-legged centipede that looks like an enormous spider but with far too many legs—up to 30.

7 BAD MOVIE TITLES

1. **Killer Tomatoes Eat France!**

2. **DON'T WORRY, WE'LL THINK OF A TITLE**

3. **RRRrrr!**

4. **The Dead Hate the Living!**

5. **PHIFFT**

6. **The Incredibly Strange Creatures Who Stopped Living and Became Mixed-up Zombies**

7. **DUDE, WHERE'S MY CAR?**

THE *Moons* of Jupiter

Jupiter is a huge planet, and it has an awful lot of moons—scientists think there are 79 altogether. The four biggest moons are Io, Europa, Ganymede, and Callisto, and 49 other moons have been given names too. Scientists are especially excited about Europa because of its potential for life. Here are all 53 named moons of Jupiter:

**Adrastea Aitne Amalthea Ananke Aoede Arche
Autonoe Callirrhoe Callisto Carme Carpo Chaldene
Cyllene Dia Elara Erinome Euanthe Eukelade Euporie
Europa Eurydome Ganymede Harpalyke Hegemone
Helike Hermippe Herse Himalia Io Iocaste Isonoe
Jupiter LI Jupiter LII Kale Kallichore Kalyke Kore
Leda Lysithea Megaclite Metis Mneme Orthosie
Pasiphae Pasithee Praxidike Sinope
Sponde Taygete Thebe Thelxinoe
Themisto Thyone**

8 POISONOUS AND VENOMOUS ANIMALS

The difference between poisonous and venomous animals is that venomous creatures inject poison, for example through a sting, while poisonous creatures have poison in their body, which can affect another animal if it eats or touches them.

POISONOUS
- Golden poison frog
- Pufferfish
- Cane toad
- Pitohui bird

VENOMOUS
- Inland taipan snake
- Duck-billed platypus
- Deathstalker scorpion
- Lonomia obliqua (silkworm moth)

⑧ Facts About the
Roman Empire
....

1. The city of Rome started off small, but by 265 BCE it had conquered all of Italy.

2. The Roman Empire was at its biggest in 117 CE, at the end of the reign of Emperor Trajan and the beginning of Emperor Hadrian's. It stretched right around the Mediterranean Sea, into the Middle East, North Africa, and as far north as Britain. It measured 2,500 mi (4,023km) from east to west.

3. Emperor Hadrian set frontiers and gave up some land in the Middle East because the Empire had become too big to manage.

4. At the Empire's frontiers, the Romans built forts to keep out hostile tribes. The strongest was Hadrian's Wall in northern Britain.

5. When the Romans conquered new land they encouraged the conquered people to accept Roman ways of life, but allowed them to worship their own gods and keep their own customs. Conquered people could become Roman citizens and join the Roman Army.

6. People who lived outside the Roman Empire—known as barbarians by the Romans—often traded with the Romans. Sometimes the Romans paid them money to stop them from attacking the Empire.

7. At the end of the 200s CE the Empire was divided into the Western Roman Empire and the Eastern Roman Empire.

8. The Western Roman Empire ended in 476 when it was attacked by barbarians, but the Eastern Roman Empire, ruled from Constantinople (now Istanbul), lasted another thousand years.

19 Unusual CRISP FLAVORS

1. **Mint Mischief**   2. Cinnamon Bun   3. **Brie**
4. Turkey and Maple Syrup   5. **Blueberry**   6. Avocado Salad
7. **Haggis and Cracked Black Pepper**   8. Broccoli
9. **Cajun Squirrel**   10. Milk Chocolate
11. **Cheshire Cheese, Red Wine, and Cranberry**   12. Beet Soup
13. **Camembert**   14. Smoked Pheasant and Wild Mushroom
15. **Cappuccino**   16. Hedgehog   17. **Crab**
18. White Stilton and Cranberry Relish
19. **Pepsi Cola and Chicken**

5 Longest Bones in the Human Body

1. **Thigh bone (femur)** –about 19 in (48cm)

2. Shin bone (tibia) –about 17 in (43cm)

3. **Back lower leg bone (fibula)** –about 16 in (40cm)

4. Upper arm bone (humerus) –about 15 in (38cm)

5. Inner lower arm (ulna) –about 11 in (28cm)

3 Smallest BONES IN THE Human Body

These bones are known as ossicles and they really are tiny. They're all found in the inner ear, and vibrate when a sound wave strikes the eardrum.

1. **Hammer (malleus)** –about 0.3 in (7.6mm)

2. Anvil (incus)–about 0.2 in (5mm)

3. **Stirrup (stapes)** –about 0.1 in (2.5mm)

16

5 Sweets *from* Charlie and the Chocolate Factory

Roald Dahl's book was inspired by his schooldays, when Cadbury's chocolate factory asked children at his school to taste and rate some of their chocolate bars.

1. Wonka's Whipple-Scrumptious Fudgemallow Delight
The Wonka Bar, in which Charlie finds his Golden Ticket.

2. Everlasting Gobstoppers
They last a very, very long time.

3. Fizzy Lifting Drinks
Drink one and float up into the air.

4. Square Candies that Look Round
Find out how in Chapter 23 of the book.

5. Swudge
Grass made of minty sugar.

17 Kinds *of* Penguins

1. **Adelie**
2. African
3. **Chinstrap**
4. Emperor
5. **Erect-crested**
6. Fiordland
7. **Galápagos**
8. Gentoo
9. **Humboldt**
10. King
11. **Little Blue**
12. Macaroni
13. **Magellanic**
14. Rockhopper
15. **Royal**
16. Snares
17. **Yellow-eyed**

There are 17 different penguin species in the world today. They all live in the southern half of the world—the Southern Hemisphere—except one, the Galápagos Penguin, which decided to be a bit different and sometimes hops over the equator to the Northern Hemisphere.

14
Very Long
TRAIN TRIPS

1. **Trans-Siberian: Moscow to Vladivostok, Russia** 5,753 mi (9,258km)

2. The Canadian: Toronto to Vancouver, Canada **2,775 mi (4,465km)**

3. **Shanghai to Lhasa, China** 2,717 mi (4,372km)

4. Indian Pacific: Sydney to Perth, Australia **2,704 mi (4,352km)**

5. **Vivek Express: Dibrugarh to Kanyakumari, India** 2,633 mi (4,237km)

6. California Zephyr: Emeryville to Chicago, US **2,438 mi (3,923km)**

7. **Paris-Moscow Express: France, Germany, Poland, Belarus, and Russia** 1,998 mi (3,199km)

8. The Ghan: Darwin to Adelaide, Australia **1,851 mi (2,979km)**

9. **Eastern and Oriental Express: Bangkok to Singapore** 1,355 mi (2,180km)

10. Blue Train: Pretoria to Cape Town, South Africa **1,000 mi (1,609km)**

11. **Osaka to Sapporo, Japan** 937 mi (1,507km)

12. Stockholm, Sweden, to Narvik, Norway **910 mi (1,464km)**

13. **Aberdeen to Penzance, UK** 722 mi (1,161km)

14. Alexandria to Aswan, Egypt **683 mi (1,099km)**

12 Birthstones

One for every month of the year, and some months have a choice.

1. **January—Garnet**
2. February—Amethyst
3. **March—Aquamarine or Bloodstone**
4. April—Diamond
5. **May—Emerald**
6. June—Pearl, Alexandrite or Moonstone
7. **July—Ruby**
8. August—Peridot, Sardonyx, or Spinel
9. **September—Sapphire**
10. October—Opal or Tourmaline
11. **November—Topaz or Citrine**
12. December—Tanzanite, Zircon, or Turquoise

8 Japanese Martial Arts

1. **Aikido** 2. Judo 3. **Jujutsu**
4. Karate 5. **Kendo**
6. Kenjutsu 7. **Sumo**
8. Taido

15 Unusual Museums

1. **Cancun Underwater Museum, Mexico**
2. Museum of Bad Art, Massachusetts, US
3. **Dog Collar Museum, Kent, UK**
4. Sulabh International Museum of Toilets, New Delhi, India
5. **Cockroach Hall of Fame, Plano, Texas, US**
6. Amsterdam Cheese Museum, The Netherlands
7. **The Underwear Museum, Wallonia, Belgium**
8. The Brain Museum, Lima, Peru
9. **Museum of Ice Cream, New York and San Francisco, US**
10. The Momofuku Ando Instant Ramen Museum, Osaka, Japan
11. **The Derwent Pencil Museum, Keswick, UK**
12. Avanos Hair Museum, Turkey
13. **Museum of Trash, New York, US**
14. The Strawberry Museum, Namur, Belgium
15. **Clowns' Gallery and Museum, London, UK**

6 of the World's Smelliest Cheeses

1. VIEUX BOULOGNE
From northern France, this was judged by an "electronic nose" to be the smelliest cheese in the world. The cheese's rind is soaked in beer for several weeks to give it its unique smell.

2. EPOISSES DE BOURGOGNE
This cheese is banned on the French public transportation system because of its odor.

3. LIMBURGER
Popular in Germany, Belgium, and the Netherlands. Bacteria on the rind account for its smell.

4. STINKING BISHOP
The rind of this English cheese is washed in fermented pear juice. It is thought to be Britain's smelliest cheese.

5. ALDEON
From northern Spain, this blue cheese is wrapped in leaves for two or three months.

6. MUNSTER D'ALSACE
The rind of this cheese is washed in wine, and the cheese is aged in humid caves in the Alsace region of northern France.

28 ROMAN Numerals

Roman numbers can get really complicated. For example, 399 is CCCXC1X. Figure out the year you were born using these Roman numerals.

I	1		
II	2		
III	3	LX	60
IV	4	LXX	70
V	5	LXXX	80
VI	6	XC	90
VII	7	C	100
VIII	8	CC	200
IX	9	CCC	300
X	10	CD	400
XX	20	D	500
XXX	30	DC	600
XL	40	DCC	700
L	50	DCCC	800
		CM	900
		M	1,000

4 Facts About PENGUINS

1. The biggest penguin is the Emperor Penguin, which can be 51 in (130cm) tall and weigh 100 lb (45kg).

2. At the other end of the scale, four Little Blue Penguins would have to stand on one another's shoulders to be as tall as one Emperor Penguin.

3. Macaroni Penguins are one of six types of crested penguins, which all have striking yellow crests. The show-offs!

4. Not all penguins live in cold places: African Penguins have to cope with high temperatures on the coasts of Namibia and South Africa.

13 Flowers You Can Eat*

1. **Alpine pinks (Dianthus)**
2. Chrysanthemum (Chrysanthemum)
3. **Daisy (Bellis perennis)**
4. Elderflower (Sambucus nigra)
5. **Hibiscus (Hibiscus rosa-sinensis)**
6. Lavender (Lavandula angustifolia)
7. **Nasturtium (Tropaeolum majus)**
8. Pot marigold (Calendula officinalis)
9. **Primrose (Primula vulgaris)**
10. Rose (Rosa)
11. **Sunflower (Helianthus annuus)**
12. Sweet violet (Viola odorata)
13. **Tiger lily
(Lilium leucanthemum var. tigrinum)**

*ask an adult before eating any flowers

Most Common SURNAMES Around the World

1. **Argentina–Fernandez**
2. Brazil–Silva
3. **Chile–Gonzalez**
4. China–Wong or Wang
5. **Denmark–Nielsen**
6. Egypt–Mohamed
7. France–Martin
8. **India–Singh**
9. Ireland–Murphy
10. **Italy–Rossi or Russo**
11. Japan–Sato
12. **Morocco–Alaoui**
13. The Netherlands –De Jong
14. **Norway–Hansen**
15. Poland–Nowak
16. **Portugal–Silva**
17. South Africa –Naidoo
18. **Spain–Garcia**
19. Sweden –Andersson
20. **Turkey–Yilmaz**
21. UAE and Saudi Arabia–Khan
22. **UK–Smith**
23. US–Smith

STEAM-POWERED CARS

Steam power was once a serious alternative to gasoline or diesel engines.

1. FARDIER À VAPEUR

Built in 1769, this was the very first automobile.

2. THE RUNABOUT

This was the first steam-powered car available for purchase. A Runabout made in 1900 was sold in 2014 for $41,000!

3. STANLEY STEAMER ROCKET

This steam-powered car set a land-speed record of 127 mph (204km/h) in 1906!

4. INSPIRATION

Steam enthusiasts continued to build and drive steam-powered cars long after they had gone out of fashion. In 2009 one of them broke the Stanley Steamer Rocket's speed record for a steam-powered car, set 103 years earlier. Its speed was 140 mph (225km/h).

12 SIGNS of the Zodiac

12. Pisces, the fish

11. Aquarius, the water carrier

10. Capricorn, the goat

9. Sagittarius, the archer

8. Scorpio, the scorpion

7. Libra, the scales

1. **Aries, the ram**

2. Taurus, the bull

3. **Gemini, the twins**

4. Cancer, the crab

5. **Leo, the lion**

6. Virgo, the virgin

9 Strange SUPERSTITIONS

1. **In France, stepping in dog poop is good luck if you step in it with your right foot, bad luck if you step in it with your left.**

2. A Lithuanian superstition says that whistling indoors summons demons.

3. **In Britain, putting new shoes on the table is supposed to bring bad luck.**

4. A Turkish superstition says that if your right hand itches you'll come into some money, but if your left hand itches you'll lose money.

5. **If you say the same word at the same time as someone else, it's considered bad luck in Italy. To undo the bad luck, touch your nose right away.**

6. In Rwanda, eating goat meat is supposed to make hair grow on your face.

7. **In many countries, Friday the 13th is thought to be unlucky. In South America and Greece, Tuesdays are unlucky, and especially Tuesday 13th.**

8. Cutting your nails after dark is unlucky in some Asian countries.

9. **Horseshoes are lucky in many countries. If you hang one above your door, make sure the ends are pointing upward to stop the luck from running out.**

The Big 5 AFRICAN SAFARI ANIMALS

These African animals are known as the Big Five
—the ones people on safari hope to see.

1. Rhinoceros (both black and white species of African rhinos)
2. AFRICAN ELEPHANT
3. Cape buffalo
4. AFRICAN LION
5. African leopard

7 African Vultures

These majestic, flying garbage collectors need our help —many are endangered.

1. **Hooded Vulture**
2. White-backed Vulture
3. **White-headed Vulture**
4. Palmnut Vulture
5. **Lappet-faced Vulture**
6. Bearded Vulture
7. **Egyptian Vulture**

9 Deadly Diseases

These diseases are caused by germs or parasites, and they are all deadly.

1. **BLACK FEVER**–caused by parasites transmitted by a sandfly bite.

2. **RABIES**–caused by bacteria from the bite of an animal infected by rabies.

3. **SLEEPING SICKNESS**–caused by parasites transmitted by a tsetse fly bite.

4. **EBOLA**–caused by a virus spread by the body fluids of an infected person.

5. **CHOLERA**–caused by bacteria from an infected person's waste products transmitted in food or water.

6. **MALARIA**–caused by parasites transmitted by a mosquito bite.

7. **TYPHUS**–caused by body lice carrying the typhus bacteria.

8. **YELLOW FEVER**–caused by the bite of a particular type of mosquito.

9. **BOTULISM**–caused by bacteria in contaminated food or in soil-infected wounds.

5 Facts About Farts

1. Farts are caused by gas-making bacteria in our insides, and also by air we swallow when we eat and drink.

2. Farts are mostly made up of gases that don't smell. Less than one percent is smelly . . . but sometimes it's very smelly.

3. **On average, in one day an adult farts about enough gas to blow up a party balloon.**

4. In Cameroon, the Komas tribe have a dance competition that involves lots of farting. The loudest, longest farts win.

5. **Scientists who study farts are called flatologists.**

5 Fart Gases

1. **Nitrogen, which makes up most of the air we breathe, can react with other chemicals to make two stinky compounds called indole and skatole.**

2. Carbon dioxide, the same gas you breathe out, which doesn't smell.

3. **Hydrogen, which mixes with sulfur to make the smelly gas hydrogen sulfide.**

4. Methane, which is highly flammable. Not all farts contain methane.

5. **Oxygen, which is in farts as a result of swallowing air.**

10
Winter Sports

1. **Curling**
2. Alpine skiing
3. **Bobsledding**
4. Snowboarding
5. **Luge**
6. Speed skating
7. **Cross-country skiing**
8. Ski jumping
9. **Ice hockey**
10. Figure skating

5 Limited Edition Cars

There aren't many of these cars around—only a few were ever made, and in one case only one was ever made.

1. **Maybach Exelero**
   Number made: 1

2. **Koenigsegg CCXR Trevita**
   Number made: 3

3. **Pagani Zonda Cinque**
   Number made: 5

4. **Ferrari Pininfarina Sergio**
   Number made: 6

5. **W Motors Lykan Hypersport**
   Number made: 7

12
Things That Have Been Used as Money

1. **Solid blocks of tea leaves—China, Mongolia, and Russia**

2. Iron nails—Scotland

3. **Shells—all over the world**

4. Knives—China

5. **Salt—many parts of the world**

6. Rum—Australia

7. **Coils of feathers—Pacific islands**

8. Rai stones (large stones with a hole in the middle) —South Pacific islands

9. **Pepper—Europe**

10. Dogs' teeth—New Guinea

11. **Whales' teeth—Fiji**

12. Parmesan cheese—Italy

Washington
–Olympia

Montana
–Helena

North Dakota
–Bismarck

Oregon
–Salem

Idaho
–Boise

Wyoming
–Cheyenne

South Dakota
–Pierre

Nevada
–Carson City

Utah–Salt
Lake City

Colorado
–Denver

Nebraska
–Lincoln

Kansas
–Topeka

California
–Sacramento

Arizona
–Phoenix

New Mexico
–Santa Fe

Oklahoma
–Oklahoma
City

Texas
–Austin

Alaska
–Juneau

Hawaii
–Honolulu

Minnesota
–St. Paul

Wisconsin
–Madison

Iowa
–Des Moines

Michigan
–Lansing

Illinois
–Springfield

Indiana
–Indianapolis

Ohio
–Columbus

Missouri
–Jefferson City

Kentucky
–Frankfort

Tennessee–Nashville

Arkansas
–Little Rock

Mississippi
–Jackson

Alabama
–Montgomery

Louisiana
–Baton Rouge

Georgia
–Atlanta

Florida
–Tallahassee

New
Hampshire
–Concord

Maine
–Augusta

Vermont
–Montpelier

New York
–Albany

Massachusetts
–Boston

Rhode Island
–Providence

Pennsylvania
–Harrisburg

Connecticut
–Hartford

West Virginia
–Charleston

Virginia
–Richmond

New Jersey
–Trenton

Delaware
–Dover

Maryland
–Annapolis

North Carolina
–Raleigh

South
Carolina
–Columbia

50

US States
and Their
Capitals

8 SUPER-FAST Animals

1. Peregrine Falcon
The fastest creature on the planet, this bird achieves speeds of more than 200 mph (322km/h) as it dives down to catch prey.

2. White-throated Needletail
Another speedy bird, this swift zooms along (horizontally) at more than 110 mph (177km/h).

3. Cheetah
The fastest land animal, the cheetah can run at 70 mph (113km/h) for short periods.

4. Sailfish
The sailfish is the fastest thing in water, at 68 mph (109km/h).

5. Pronghorn antelope
Not as fast as the cheetah, but in a long-distance race the pronghorn would win—it can run at 61 mph (98km/h) for long periods.

6. Mako shark
The mako glides through the sea a bit behind the sailfish, at 60 mph (97km/h).

7. Ostrich
This big bird is the fastest bird on land—it's way behind the swift at 45 mph (72km/h).

8. Dragonfly
The fastest insect, clocked at 35 mph (56km/h).

15 AMAZING Prehistoric Animals

1. GIGANTOPITHECUS
The largest ape that ever lived, it weighed up to 1,000 lb (454kg), but died out 100,000 years ago.

2. MEGATHERIUM
Looked like a modern tree sloth, but was as tall as a giraffe when it stood on its hind legs. It died out 8,000 years ago.

3. MEGALODON
The biggest shark ever, this massive predator ruled the seas until around 1.6 million years ago.

4. EPIGAULUS
A horned rodent that lived in burrows. It died out around 5 million years ago.

5. PACACERATHERIUM
The largest land mammal that's ever lived. It died out around 25 million years ago.

6. TITANOBOA
This snake was 48 ft (15m) long and 5 ft (1.5m) thick. It died out 60 million years ago.

7. DOEDICURUS
This armadillo-like animal weighed 1.5 tons. It died out 15,000 years ago.

8. WOOLLY MAMMOTH
These shaggy elephant-like animals had thick fur to protect them from the cold. Most died out around 10,000 years ago.

9. GIANT PACARANA
A rodent the size of a cow that weighed a ton. It died out 2 million years ago.

10. ARCHELON
A gigantic turtle weighing 2.4 tons. It died out 65 million years ago.

11. ANDREWSARCHUS
Probably the largest meat-eating mammal ever, up to 20 ft (6m) long, 7 ft (2m) tall, and a ton in weight. It died out around 35 million years ago.

12. GIGANOTOSAURUS
As far as we know, the biggest land predator of all time, 43 ft (13m) long and 14 tons in weight. It died out around 97 million years ago.

13. SMILODON
A saber-toothed cat with canine teeth 8 in (20cm) long. It died out around 10,000 years ago.

14. JAEKELOPTERUS
A huge sea scorpion 7 ft (2m) long with claws 18 in (46cm) long. It died out around 390 million years ago.

15. WOOLLY RHINOCEROS
A furry Ice Age rhino with a 3-ft (1-m) long horn. It died out 10,000 years ago.

6 Facts about Fungi

. . . .

1. Living things are divided into plants, animals, bacteria, and fungi. You might think that a mushroom is very similar to a plant, but in fact fungi are more closely related to animals than to plants.

2. Like animals, but unlike plants, fungi eat food. They always live on or near their food.

3. Fungi don't need light as plants do—they are often found in dark places.

4. Fungi include mushrooms, molds, and yeasts—there are more than 1.5 million species.

5. Fungi can cure disease —the antibiotic penicillin is a fungus. They're also responsible for causing diseases in people and plants.

6. Fungi help break down decaying matter, and do all sorts of other vital jobs.

9 Cures
for the
Black Death

The Black Death was probably an outbreak of bubonic plague. In the Middle Ages, it killed up to half of the population of Europe. As if things weren't bad enough, these were some of the "cures."

1. **Take the poisons arsenic or mercury.**

2. Strap a live chicken next to the sores on the body.

3. **Cut open a vein to get rid of "bad blood."**

4. Attach leeches to your body to suck your blood.

5. **Drink a mixture of powdered roasted eggshells, crushed marigolds, beer, and molasses.**

6. Eat crushed emeralds.

7. **Drink your own wee twice a day.**

8. Apply a mixture of human poop, flowers, and onions to sores.

9. **Drink the dissolved powdered horn of a unicorn. (The tusks of whales called narwhals were sold as unicorn horns for ten times their weight in gold.)**

5 AMAZING AMAZON Animal World Records

1. **The titan beetle, the world's biggest beetle.**

2. The harpy eagle, the world's biggest eagle.

3. **The pygmy marmoset, the world's smallest monkey.**

4. The pirarucu, the world's largest freshwater fish.

5. **The howler monkey, the world's loudest land animal.**

10 Gases in EARTH'S ATMOSPHERE

1. **Nitrogen–78.08%**
2. Oxygen–20.95%
3. **Argon–0.93%**

Teeny-tiny amounts of the following gases:

4. Carbon dioxide
5. **Neon**
6. Hydrogen
7. **Helium**
8. Methane
9. **Nitrous oxide**
10. Ozone

As well as these gases, the air contains varying amounts of water vapor. The percentages in the list are for dry air.

8 Tallest Waterfalls in the World

1. **Angel Falls, Venezuela– 3,212 ft (979m)**
2. Tugela Falls, South Africa– 3,110 ft (948m)
3. **Tres Hermanas Falls, Peru– 2,999 ft (914m)**
4. Olo'upena Falls, Hawaii, US– 2,953 ft (900m)
5. **Yumbilla Falls, Peru– 2,940 ft (896m)**
6. Vinnufossen, Norway – 2,822 ft (860m)
7. **Balaifossen, Norway– 2,789 ft (850m)**
8. Pu'uka'oku Falls, Hawaii, US– 2,756 ft (840m)

The 5 Great Lakes

1. **Lake Superior–31,820 mi² (82,414km²)**
2. Lake Huron–23,010 mi² (59,596km²)
3. **Lake Michigan–22,410 mi² (58,016km²)**
4. Lake Erie–9,930 mi² (25,719km²)
5. **Lake Ontario–7,520 mi² (19,477km²)**

These freshwater lakes lie on the border between the US and Canada (Lake Michigan lies within the US).

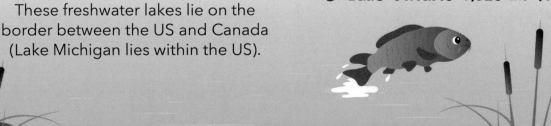

33

8 Planets in Our Solar System

There are eight planets in our solar system. Here they are, from the closest to the Sun to the farthest away. An easy way to remember the order is to use a sentence in which each word starts with the first letter of the planet—for example, **Men Very Easily Make Jars Serve Useful Needs.** The four planets closest to the Sun are rocky, the other four are giant gassy planets.

SUN

1. Mercury

2. Venus

3. Earth

4. Mars

8. Neptune

7. Uranus

5. Jupiter

6. Saturn

3 Types of Galaxies

There are three main types of galaxies in the universe. Our galaxy, the Milky Way, is a spiral galaxy. There are lots of different kinds of each type.

1. SPIRAL GALAXIES

2. ELLIPTICAL GALAXIES—shaped like a stretched-out ball

3. IRREGULAR GALAXIES

7 Creepy-crawly FACTS About COCKROACHES

1. **Cockroaches have white blood.**

2. There are more than 50,000 different kinds.

3. **They can run about as fast as you can walk.**

4. They eat anything—soap, glue, their own cast-off skin, and sometimes each other.

5. **The Madagascan Giant Hissing Cockroach is often kept as a pet.**

6. The giant burrowing cockroach, which lives in Australia, is the world's heaviest cockroach. It weighs 1.2 oz (35g) and measures up to $3\frac{1}{8}$ in (8cm) long.

7. **The world's largest cockroach, Megaloblatta longipennis, lives in South America. it measures up to $3\frac{3}{4}$ in (9.7cm) long and $1\frac{3}{4}$ in (4.5cm) across, with a wingspan of up to $7\frac{3}{4}$ in (20cm).**

8 RULERS with Unflattering Nicknames

The Spanish region of León seems to have been an unflattering nickname hotspot.

1. **Sancho the Fat, King of León**

2. Ordoño the Wicked, King of León

3. **Alfonso the Slobberer, King of León**

4. Ivaylo the Cabbage, Czar of Bulgaria

5. **Charles the Bald, King of France**

6. Louis Do-Nothing, King of France

7. **Joanna the Mad, Queen of Spain**

8. Charles the Mad, King of France

12 Popular Breeds of Cats

1. **Abyssinian**
2. American Bobtail
3. **Bengal**
4. Burmese
5. **Egyptian Mau**
6. Maine Coon 7. **Manx**
8. Norwegian Forest
9. Persian 10. **Ragdoll**
11. Scottish Fold
12. **Tonkinese**

8

Types of Bears

There are only eight types of bears in the world today, or nine if you include grizzly-polar bear hybrids.

1. AMERICAN BLACK BEAR
—the most common bear species in the world.

2. ASIAN BLACK BEAR
—also known as moon bears or white-chested bears.

3. BROWN BEAR
—this species includes grizzly bears.

4. GIANT PANDA
—possibly the cutest kind of bear.

5. SLOTH BEAR
—eats insects and lives in South Asia.

6. SUN BEAR
—lives in tropical rain forests in Southeast Asia and is sometimes called the honey bear, after its favorite food.

7. POLAR BEAR
—along with a type of brown bear called the Kodiak bear, the polar bear is the largest land predator in the world (although it is sometimes classified as a marine mammal as it spends a lot of time on sea ice).

8. SPECTACLED BEAR
—also known as the Andean bear, the only type of bear that lives in South America.

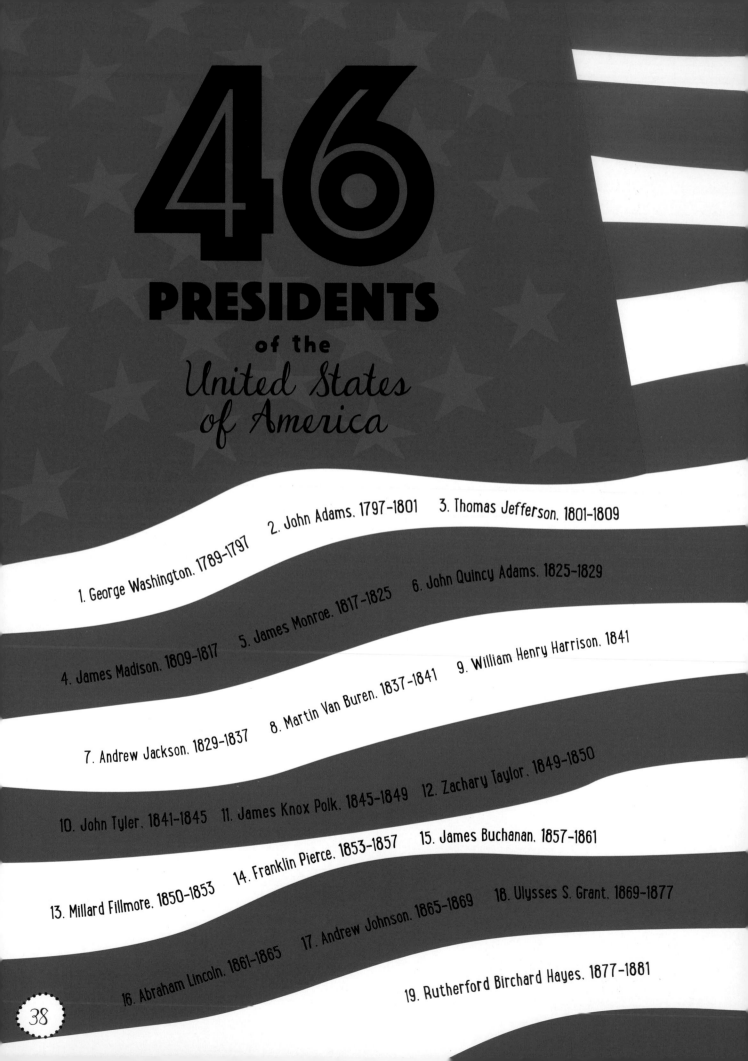

46

PRESIDENTS

of the

United States of America

1. George Washington, 1789–1797   2. John Adams, 1797–1801   3. Thomas Jefferson, 1801–1809

4. James Madison, 1809–1817   5. James Monroe, 1817–1825   6. John Quincy Adams, 1825–1829

7. Andrew Jackson, 1829–1837   8. Martin Van Buren, 1837–1841   9. William Henry Harrison, 1841

10. John Tyler, 1841–1845   11. James Knox Polk, 1845–1849   12. Zachary Taylor, 1849–1850

13. Millard Fillmore, 1850–1853   14. Franklin Pierce, 1853–1857   15. James Buchanan, 1857–1861

16. Abraham Lincoln, 1861–1865   17. Andrew Johnson, 1865–1869   18. Ulysses S. Grant, 1869–1877

19. Rutherford Birchard Hayes, 1877–1881

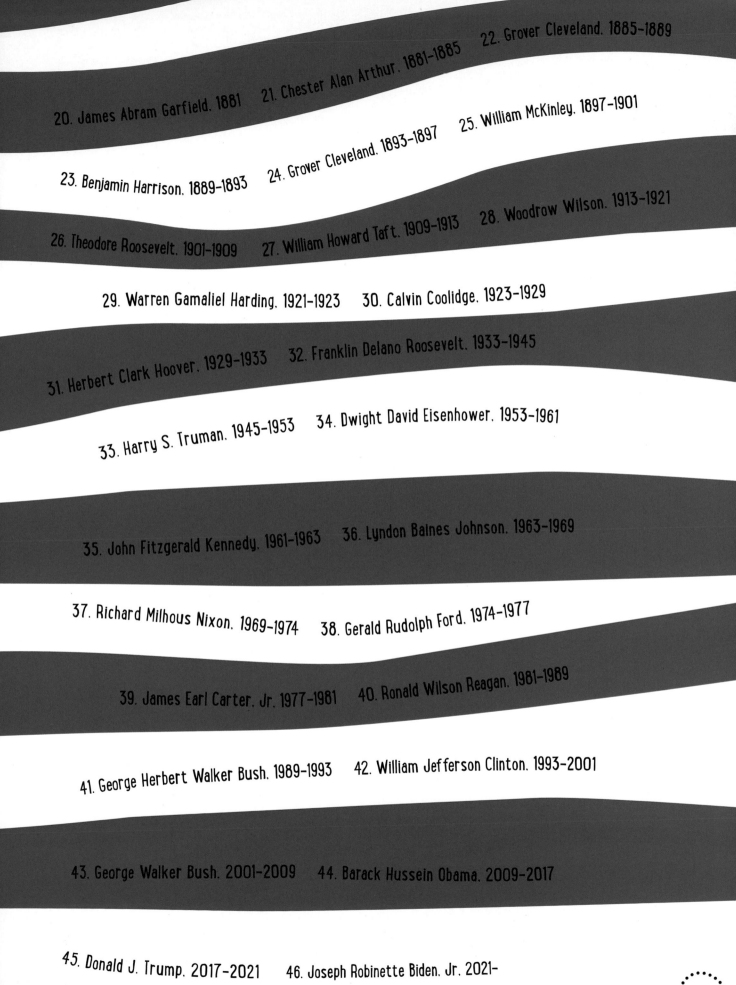

20. James Abram Garfield. 1881   21. Chester Alan Arthur. 1881–1885   22. Grover Cleveland. 1885–1889

23. Benjamin Harrison. 1889–1893   24. Grover Cleveland. 1893–1897   25. William McKinley. 1897–1901

26. Theodore Roosevelt. 1901–1909   27. William Howard Taft. 1909–1913   28. Woodrow Wilson. 1913–1921

29. Warren Gamaliel Harding. 1921–1923   30. Calvin Coolidge. 1923–1929

31. Herbert Clark Hoover. 1929–1933   32. Franklin Delano Roosevelt. 1933–1945

33. Harry S. Truman. 1945–1953   34. Dwight David Eisenhower. 1953–1961

35. John Fitzgerald Kennedy. 1961–1963   36. Lyndon Baines Johnson. 1963–1969

37. Richard Milhous Nixon. 1969–1974   38. Gerald Rudolph Ford. 1974–1977

39. James Earl Carter. Jr. 1977–1981   40. Ronald Wilson Reagan. 1981–1989

41. George Herbert Walker Bush. 1989–1993   42. William Jefferson Clinton. 1993–2001

43. George Walker Bush. 2001–2009   44. Barack Hussein Obama. 2009–2017

45. Donald J. Trump. 2017–2021   46. Joseph Robinette Biden. Jr. 2021–

7 ◆ Ghost Towns

. . . .

Ghost towns are villages, towns, or cities that
have been completely abandoned by people.
Who knows, maybe some of them are haunted . . .

1. PRIPYAT, UKRAINE
Pripyat was home to 50,000 people before an accident at
the Chernobyl Nuclear Power Station meant that the town had
to be abandoned because of high levels of radiation.

2. BODIE, CALIFORNIA, US

People flocked to Bodie in search of gold in the 1800s,
and at one time 10,000 people lived there. Today,
its ramshackle buildings are a tourist attraction.

3. CRACO, ITALY
This hillside town was abandoned because of landslides, flooding,
and an earthquake in 1980, when the last people moved out.

4. KOLMANSKOP, NAMIBIA
Kolmanskop was founded in the early 1900s by
German diamond miners, but later abandoned.

5. HASHIMA ISLAND, JAPAN
Originally inhabited because of coal mining,
5,200 people were once crammed onto the tiny island.
In 1974 mining stopped and the island was abandoned.

6. VAROSHA, CYPRUS
This beachside town was one of the most popular vacation
destinations in the world, with a population of 39,000. It was
abandoned in 1974 when Turkey invaded Cyprus.

7. CONSONNO, ITALY
The original village was bought by a property developer,
who moved everyone out and built a new town, but it was
abandoned after a landslide in 1976. Today, it hosts the
Hide and Seek World Championships.

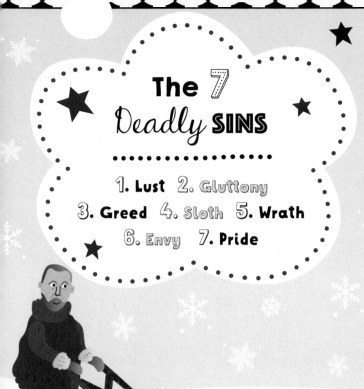

The 7 Deadly SINS

1. **Lust** 2. *Gluttony*
3. **Greed** 4. *Sloth* 5. **Wrath**
6. **Envy** 7. **Pride**

8 THINGS THAT HAVE BEEN FOUND in Sharks' Stomachs

1. **Deer antlers (and entire deer)**
2. Car license plate
3. **Bottle of wine**
4. Video camera
5. **Suit of armor**
6. Fur coat
7. **Cans of food**
8. Cannonball

10 INTREPID Explorers

1. Roald Amundsen
The first person to reach the South Pole.

2. Christopher Columbus
Sailed across the Atlantic to the Caribbean in 1492, opening up a whole New World for the Europeans.

3. Amelia Earhart
The first woman to fly solo over the Atlantic and Pacific Oceans.

4. Captain James Cook
Sailed twice around the world, mapping thousands of miles of previously uncharted land.

5. Leif Erikson
Viking explorer who sailed across the Atlantic 500 years before Columbus.

6. Meriwether Lewis and William Clark
The first settlers to travel across the continent of North America.

7. Ferdinand Magellan
The first person to sail all the way around the world.

8. Marco Polo
Traveled from Venice in Italy to China, and stayed at the court of Kublai Khan.

9. Vasco da Gama
Sailed around Africa and opened a new trade route from Europe to Asia.

10. Robert Scott
Antarctic explorer who was beaten to the South Pole by Amundsen and died on his final expedition.

10 *of the* World's Biggest Islands

In case you're wondering why Australia isn't at the top of this list, it's not included because it's a continental landmass. But it is also an enormous island—2,941,514 mi² (7,618,493 km²).

1. **Greenland—840,003 mi² (2,175,600km²)**
2. New Guinea—303,381 mi² (785,753km²)
3. **Borneo—288,869 mi² (748,168km²)**
4. Madagascar—226,917 mi² (587,713km²)
5. **Baffin, Canada—194,574 mi² (503,944km²)**
6. Sumatra, Indonesia—171,069 mi² (443,066km²)
7. **Honshu, Japan—87,182 mi² (225,800km²)**
8. Great Britain—88,787 mi² (229,957km²)
9. **Victoria, Canada—85,154 mi² (220,548km²)**
10. Ellesmere, Canada—71,029 mi² (183,965km²)

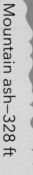

1. **Coast redwood—381 ft**
2. Mountain ash—328 ft
3. **Coast Douglas fir—328 ft**
4. Sitka spruce—318 ft
5. **Giant sequoia—315 ft**
6. Yellow meranti—305 ft
7. **Manna gum—299 ft**
8. Southern blue gum—299 ft
9. **Alpine ash—289 ft**
10. Brown top stringbark—282 ft
11. **Mengaris—282 ft**

11 TALL *Trees*

These trees might be a bit of a challenge to climb—they're the tallest on the planet. The measurements are of the tallest ones of their kind alive today.

6 ENTICING FIRST LINES from *Famous* BOOKS

1. **"All children, except one, grow up."**
   J. M. BARRIE, *PETER PAN*

◆

2. "'Alice was beginning to get very tired of sitting by her sister on the bank, and of having nothing to do: once or twice she had peeped into the book her sister was reading, but it had no pictures or conversations in it, 'and what is the use of a book,' thought Alice, 'without pictures or conversation?'"
   LEWIS CARROLL, *ALICE'S ADVENTURES IN WONDERLAND*

◆

3. **"It was a bright cold day in April, and the clocks were striking thirteen."**
   GEORGE ORWELL, *1984*

4. "Far out in the uncharted backwaters of the unfashionable end of the Western Spiral arm of the Galaxy lies a small unregarded yellow sun."
   DOUGLAS ADAMS, *THE HITCHHIKER'S GUIDE TO THE GALAXY*

◆

5. **"Mr. and Mrs. Dursley, of number four Privet Drive, were proud to say that they were perfectly normal, thank you very much."**
   J. K. ROWLING, *HARRY POTTER AND THE SORCERER'S STONE*

◆

6. "I write this sitting in the kitchen sink."
   DODIE SMITH, *I CAPTURE THE CASTLE*

5 Prehistoric *Pterosaurs*

Pterosaurs were flying reptiles that swooped through prehistoric skies at the same time as dinosaurs roamed the land. They died out completely and aren't related to modern birds or to bats.

1. **Quetzalcoatlus, the biggest flying animal ever discovered, with a wingspan of up to 36 ft (11m).**

2. Pteranodon, a large pterosaur with a crest on its head and a wingspan of up to 23 ft (7m).

3. **Pterodaustro, a small pterosaur with a thousand long, thin, flexible teeth for filtering plankton.**

4. Dsungaripterus, a pterosaur with a hooked beak for prying out shellfish.

5. **Nemicolopterus, the smallest pterosaur discovered so far, with a wingspan of just 10 in (25cm).**

14 MEGACITIES

These cities are huge metropolitan areas and many of them sprawl for a very long way outside the city center. They have the highest populations in the world.

1. **Tokyo, Japan—38.1 million people**
2. Shanghai, China—34 million people
3. **Jakarta, Indonesia—31.5 million people**
4. Delhi, India—27.2 million people
5. **Seoul, South Korea—25.6 million people**
6. Guangzhou, China—25 million people
7. **Beijing, China—24.9 million people**
8. Manila, Philippines—24.1 million people
9. **Mumbai, India—23.9 million people**
10. New York, US—23.9 million people
11. **Shenzhen, China—23.3 million people**
12. São Paulo, Brazil—21.2 million people
13. **Mexico City, Mexico—21.1 million people**
14. Lagos, Nigeria—21 million people

4
FACTS about Cities

1. In 133 BCE, Rome became the first city in the world with more than a million people living in it.

2. La Rinconada, in the Andes mountains in Peru, is the highest settlement in the world at 16,831 ft (5,130m) above sea level.

3. London was the world's biggest city from 1825 to 1918. In 1900 it became the first city of more than 5 million people.

4. The city at most risk from rising sea levels is Malé in the Maldives, which is the flattest country in the world.

3 Dangerous Sharks

There are nearly 400 different kinds of sharks, but not many are dangerous to people. Only three species regularly attack humans—and not very often. Sharks might be scary, but many are endangered and need our protection.

1. GREAT WHITE SHARK

These whopping great sharks—up to 23 ft (7m) long—sometimes mistake people for seals.

2. BULL SHARK

Bull sharks are much smaller—around 8.2 ft (2.5m) long—but tend to stay close to the coast, where people might be swimming. They can also swim in freshwater.

3. TIGER SHARK

Tiger sharks are around 10 ft (3m) long on average, but huge ones have been spotted—up to 20 ft (6m) long. They are unfussy eaters and can be aggressive.

5 FEROCIOUS MEAT-EATING DINOSAURS

1. Megalosaurus was a Jurassic meat-eater 30 ft (9m) long. It was one of the first dinosaurs to be discovered and the first dinosaur to be named (in 1824).

2. Allosaurus was a 39-ft- (12-m-) long Jurassic predator.

3. Tyrannosaurus rex was a fearsome Cretaceous dinosaur. It measured 39 ft (12m) long, weighed 8 tons, and had 60 sharp teeth.

4. Giganotosaurus was longer than T. rex and weighed 9 tons. It lived millions of years before T. rex roamed the Earth.

5. Spinosaurus was probably the longest meat-eating dinosaur, at 59 ft (18m) from nose to tail, but it weighed half as much as Giganotosaurus.

5 STRING INSTRUMENTS in an Orchestra

1. Violin   2. Viola   **3. Cello**
4. Double Bass   **5. Harp**

List of 51 European Countries

1. Albania
2. Andorra
3. Armenia
4. Austria
5. Azerbaijan
6. Belarus
7. Belgium
8. Bosnia and Herzegovina
9. Bulgaria
10. Croatia
11. Cyprus
12. Czech Republic
13. Denmark
14. Estonia
15. Finland
16. France
17. Georgia
18. Germany
19. Greece
20. Hungary
21. Iceland
22. Ireland
23. Italy
24. Kazakhstan
25. Kosovo
26. Latvia
27. Liechtenstein
28. Lithuania
29. Luxembourg
30. Macedonia
31. Malta
32. Moldova
33. Monaco
34. Montenegro
35. Netherlands
36. Norway
37. Poland
38. Portugal
39. Romania
40. Russia
41. San Marino
42. Serbia
43. Slovakia
44. Slovenia
45. Spain
46. Sweden
47. Switzerland
48. Turkey
49. Ukraine
50. United Kingdom
51. Vatican City

5 BIG Bugs

1. **Biggest spider:** Goliath bird-eating spider, up to 12 in (30cm) across.

2. **Biggest flying insect:** Titan beetle, up to 7 in (17cm) long.

3. **Heaviest insect:** Wetapunga, up to 4 in long and weighing up to 2.5 oz (70g).

4. **Insect with the biggest wingspan:** Queen Alexandra's birdwing butterfly, up to 12 in (30cm) across.

5. **Longest insect:** Giant Chinese stick insect: up to 24 1/2 in (62.4cm) long.

8 Amazing *Australian* Animals

1. BILBY
—desert-dwelling, pointed nosed, long-eared, burrowing mammal.

2. THORNY DEVIL
—extremely spiky ant-eating lizard.

3. CASSOWARY
—blue-and-red-necked flightless bird up to 6 ½ ft (2m) tall with dangerous claws.

4. SUGAR GLIDERS
—cute sap-eating mammal that can glide up to 164 ft (50m) between trees.

5. ECHIDNA
—spiny, hedgehoglike, ant-eating, egg-laying mammal.

6. QUOKKA
—small, furry animal related to kangaroos and wallabies.

7. TASMANIAN DEVIL
—meat-eating mammal that can bite through almost anything.

8. PLATYPUS
—river-dwelling, egg-laying mammal with a bill like a duck's.

8 Dangerous Jobs *of the* Past and Present

1. Fisherman
Fishermen and -women often work in rough seas in the cold and dark, in danger of being washed overboard. Alaskan crab fishing, which happens in winter in freezing seas, is one of the most dangerous jobs in the world.

2. Ancient Roman Gladiator
Most gladiators were prisoners of war or slaves. They fought other gladiators or wild animals in front of a bloodthirsty crowd. Obviously, the chances of being killed were high.

3. Honey Gatherers
In Nepal, honey gatherers climb down steep cliffs in the foothills of the Himalaya mountain range to cut chunks of honeycomb from the nests of honey bees. The nests are between 8,200 ft (2,500m) and 13,000 ft (4,000m) high.

4. Egg Collectors

In the Arctic today, and in the past in different parts of the world, people have eaten seabirds' eggs. Egg collectors are lowered down on a rope to gather murre eggs, which are laid on ledges in the cliff face, shooing away angry birds with a free hand.

5. Lumberjack

The job of a lumberjack—cutting down, preparing, and transporting trees—has always been one of the world's most dangerous, because of the risks of chainsaws and falling trees.

6. Victorian Chimney Sweep's Apprentice

Chimney sweeps employed children as young as six, who were small enough to climb up chimneys to clean them. The children scraped their arms and legs as they climbed the chimneys, and breathed in poisonous soot that could eventually kill them.

7. Miner

Working deep underground in cramped conditions, where there's often a high risk of exploding gas, is a highly dangerous job. Mining disasters have claimed thousands of lives.

8. 18th-Century Powder Monkey

Any job in a war zone is bound to be dangerous, but being a powder monkey in the 1700s, providing gunpowder for a ship's cannons, must be one of the worst. Small adults or children had to run from the magazine, where the gunpowder was stored, back to the cannon, with a high chance that it might explode on the way.

BIGGEST Empires

1. THE BRITISH EMPIRE

In 1920, the British Empire ruled around 13.7 million mi² (35.5 million km²), and a quarter of everyone on Earth.

2. MONGOL EMPIRE

The Mongol Empire was a continuous empire, not dotted around the world like the British Empire. Most of it was conquered by Genghis Khan. It was at its biggest under Genghis Khan's grandson, Kublai Khan, in the 13th century—around 9 million mi² (24 million km²).

3. RUSSIAN EMPIRE

At 8.8 million mi² (22.8 million km²), the Russian Empire spanned three continents. It lasted until the beginning of the 20th century.

4. QING DYNASTY

Under the Qing dynasty, which lasted from 1644 to 1912, China tripled in size. At its height, it covered 5.7 million mi² (14.7 million km²).

5. SPANISH EMPIRE

Spanish explorers conquered lands in the New World in the 15th and 16th centuries, and ruled an empire of 15.3 million mi² (13.7 million km²).

4 EDIBLE Insects

Insects are high in protein and don't need lots of land to graze. Why not give some of these tasty treats a try?

1. GRASSHOPPERS
In Mexico, these are known as chapulines and are toasted and eaten as snacks, often with guacamole and tortillas.

2. WATER BUGS
These huge insects, up to 3 in (7.5cm) long, are often sold on street stalls in Southeast Asia, steamed, fried or roasted.

3. TERMITES
These are eaten in West Africa, Australia, and South America, either raw or roasted.

4. DRAGONFLIES
In Indonesia, these are eaten boiled or fried.

8 Australian States and Territories and Their Capitals

1. **New South Wales–Sydney**
2. Victoria–Melbourne
3. **QUEENSLAND–Brisbane**
4. Western Australia–Perth
5. **SOUTH AUSTRALIA–Adelaide**
6. Tasmania–Hobart
7. **AUSTRALIAN CAPITAL TERRITORY–Canberra**
8. Northern Territory–Darwin

3 BIGGEST Birds' Eggs

1. Elephant bird egg
Elephant birds are now extinct but they were enormous (almost 10 feet tall) and laid the biggest eggs of any bird we know about.

3. Ostrich egg
Today, ostriches lay the biggest egg of any bird. The world record goes to an ostrich egg that weighed more than 5 1/2 lb (2.5kg).

2. Emu egg
Emu eggs are also huge, and they're a lovely green-blue color.

How to Say 'My Name is ...' in 11 Different Languages

1. **Dutch**
Ik heet . . .

2. **FRENCH**
Je m'appelle . . .

3. **Spanish**
Me llamo . . .

4. German
Ich heisse . . .

5. **ITALIAN**
Mi chiamo . . .

6. Swedish
Jag heter . . .

7. **Swahili**
Ninaitwa . . .

8. **Hungarian**
Mi a neve . . .

9. Fijian
Na yacaqu o . . .

10. **Portuguese**
Chamo-me . . .

11. **MALAY:**
Nama saya . . .

10 Surprising Patron Saints

1. **Saint Friard, patron saint of people with a wasp phobia**

2. Saint Martin of Tours, patron saint of geese

3. **Saint Isodore of Seville, patron saint of the Internet**

4. Saint Apollonia, patron saint of dentists

5. **Saint Drogo, patron saint of unattractive people**

6. Saint Ambrose, patron saint of beekeepers

7. **Saint Genesius, patron saint of comedians and lawyers**

8. Saint Blaise, patron saint of sore throats and wool combers

9. **Saint Malo, patron saint of pigkeepers**

10. Saint Lidwina, patron saint of ice skaters

51

10 DEADLY Mushrooms TO AVOID

Some mushrooms are so poisonous they can kill. They have suitably deadly names, but many of them look very similar to edible mushrooms. Never pick mushrooms unless you are a mushroom expert—you might be picking one of these . . .

1. **Death cap**
2. Webcap
3. **Autumn skullcap**
4. Destroying angel
5. **Deadly dapperling**
6. Fool's mushroom
7. **Death angel**
8. Deadly parasol
9. **Funeral bell**
10. Angel's wings

5 Most Widely Spoken Languages

1. **MANDARIN:** about 908 million speakers

2. Spanish: about 442 million speakers

3. **ENGLISH:** about 378 million speakers

4. Hindustani: about 274 million speakers

5. **ARABIC:** about 274 million speakers

5 Jokes About Cheese

1. **What cheese can be used to hide a horse?**
Mascarpone.

2. **What happened when the cheese factory exploded?**
De brie went everywhere.

3. **How do you get a mouse to smile?**
Say cheese.

4. **What do you call cheese that isn't yours?**
Nacho cheese.

5. **What cheese surrounds a castle?**
Moatsarella.

13 ANCIENT GREEK CITY-STATES

Ancient Greece wasn't a country, but a collection of city-states that all had their own cultures. The most famous are Athens and Sparta, which were at war with one another for nearly 30 years. There were more than a thousand Ancient Greek city-states, scattered all over what's now Greece and the Mediterranean coasts of other countries. Here are some of the most important.

1. **Argos**   2. Athens   3. **Chalcis**
4. Corinth   5. **Delphi**   6. Ephesus
7. **Epidaurus**   8. Eretria
9. **Knossos**   10. Massalia
11. **Olympia**   12. Syracuse
13. **Thebes**

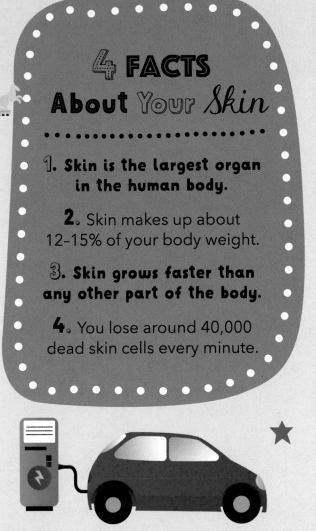

4 FACTS About Your Skin

1. **Skin is the largest organ in the human body.**

2. Skin makes up about 12-15% of your body weight.

3. **Skin grows faster than any other part of the body.**

4. You lose around 40,000 dead skin cells every minute.

3 Electric Vehicle Facts

1. The first electric vehicles were made in the 1800s, but gasoline and diesel engines became more popular.

2. Electric vehicles don't belch poisonous fumes into the atmosphere, they use energy extremely efficiently, and they're very quiet.

3. Around a quarter of greenhouse gases—which trap heat in the atmosphere and make the Earth warmer—come from vehicles that burn fossil fuels. If we can use vehicles that use electricity made from solar power, it will be better for the planet.

Famous Shipwrecks

1. RMS TITANIC is probably the most famous shipwreck of all—the passenger liner sank on its very first voyage from Southampton, UK, to New York, US, in 1912. The wreck was found 2.5 mi deep, off the coast of Newfoundland, in 1985.

2. The **S.S. REPUBLIC** was a steamship that sank in 1865 off the coast of Georgia, US. It sank full of silver and gold coins, although happily everyone aboard survived. The wreck was found in 2003, along with the treasure.

3. King Henry VIII's warship the MARY ROSE sank off the coast of southern England in 1545. It was raised from the seabed in 1982, and the 500-year-old ship can now be seen in a museum, along with thousands of artifacts from inside it that were preserved in the seabed.

4. THE WHYDAH GALLY was a pirate ship that sank off the coast of Massachusetts in 1717, full of pirate treasure. It was discovered buried in the sand in 1984, and many of its gold and silver riches have been recovered.

5. The oldest complete shipwreck ever discovered dates from 400 BCE. It's an Ancient Greek trading ship, complete with its mast and rudder, discovered 1.2 mi (2km) deep in the Black Sea in 2017.

5 Ocean zones

1. **Sunlight Zone** (0–660 ft / 0–200m)

2. **Twilight Zone** (660–3,300 ft / 200–1,000m)

3. **Midnight Zone** (3,300–13,100 ft / 1,000–4,000m)

4. **Abyssal Zone** (13,100–19,700 ft / 4,000–6,000m)

5. **Haden Zone or Trench** (19,700–36,100 ft / 6,000–11,000m)

7 Deadly Battles

These battles all had horribly high numbers of dead and wounded. They're some of the most deadly in the history of the world.

1. Battle of Plataea, 479 BCE

The last land battle in the war between the invading Persians and the allied Greek city-states.

2. Battle of Changping, 260 BCE

Won by the state of Qin, which defeated the state of Zhou. The Qin leader became China's first emperor.

3. Battle of the Catalaunian Plains, 451 CE

Fought between the Visigoths (with help from the Romans) and the Huns.

4. Battle of Didgori, 1121

The kingdom of Georgia fought the Great Seljuq Empire.

5. Third Battle of Panipat, 1761

Fought between the invading Afghan forces and the Maratha Empire.

6. Battle of the Somme, 1916

The bloodiest battle of the First World War.

7. Battle of Stalingrad, 1942–43

The biggest fight of the Second World War, which is the bloodiest war in history.

11 Unusual Competitions

1. Night of the Radishes, Oaxaca, Mexico

Every December 23, the people of Oaxaca carve radishes into amazing shapes and scenes. There's a prize for the best radish sculpture.

2. Cheese Rolling, Gloucestershire, UK

Every May, competitors chase a 10-lb wheel of Double Gloucester cheese down a steep hill. The winner gets the cheese.

3. French Pig Squealing Championships, Trie-sur-Baise, France

Contestants impersonate squealing pigs.

4. Yorkshire Pudding Boat Race, Brawby, UK

Giant-sized Yorkshire puddings, made from batter, are coated in yacht varnish and raced across a pond.

5. World Bog Snorkeling Championships, Llanwrtyd Wells, Wales, UK

Competitors snorkel through a trench cut into a peat bog. The quickest time over two lengths wins.

6. Air Guitar World Championships, Oulu, Finland

People pretend to play a guitar to music. The air guitarist judged to be the best wins a real guitar.

7. Ugly Competition, Bilbao, Spain

Every August, people compete to pull the ugliest face they can.

8. Worm Charming, Llanwrtyd Wells, Wales, UK

The grass is divided up between contestants, then they are given an hour to lure the most worms out of their patch.

9. Hide and Seek World Championships, Consonno, Italy

Players from all over the world have a minute to find a hiding space in this ghost town in northern Italy.

10. International Cherry Pit Spitting Championships, Michigan, US

The farthest pit-spitter wins.

11. Toe Wrestling Championships, Ashbourne, UK

Like thumb wrestling, but with feet.

Top Electric Car Countries

The most electric cars are sold in the US, where around 400,000 are sold each year, and in China, where around 250,000 electric cars are sold each year. But compared to the total number of cars sold in those countries, these are small numbers. The following are the countries with the most electric cars sold compared to ordinary gasoline- or diesel-engine cars.

1. NORWAY
—more than two in every ten cars sold are electric vehicles.

2. THE NETHERLANDS
—nearly one in ten cars sold is electric.

3. SWEDEN
—there's a big drop down after the Netherlands. In Sweden, fewer than three cars in every hundred are electric.

4. FRANCE
—just over one car in every hundred sold is electric.

5. UNITED KINGDOM
—the percentage is very slightly less than in France.

54 African Capitals

1. **Algeria: Algiers** 2. Angola: Luanda 3. **Benin: Porto-Novo** 4. Botswana: Gaborone 5. **Burkina Faso: Ouagadougou** 6. Burundi: Bujumbura 7. **Cabo Verde: Praia** 8. Cameroon: Yaounde 9. **Central African Republic: Bangui** 10. Chad: N'Djamena 11. **Comoros: Moroni** 12. Democratic Republic of the Congo: Kinshasa 13. **Republic of the Congo: Brazzaville** 14. Côte d'Ivoire: Yamoussoukro 15. **Djibouti: Djibouti** 16. Egypt: Cairo 17. **Equatorial Guinea: Malabo and Oyala** 18. Eritrea: Asmara 19. **Eswatini (formerly Swaziland): Mbabane and Lobamba** 20. Ethiopia: Addis Ababa 21. **Gabon: Libreville** 22. Gambia: Banjul 23. **Ghana: Accra** 24. Guinea: Conakry 25. **Guinea Bissau: Bissau** 26. Kenya: Nairobi 27. **Lesotho: Maseru** 28. Liberia: Monrovia 29. **Libya: Tripoli** 30. Madagascar: Antananarivo 31. **Malawi: Lilongwe** 32. Mali: Bamako 33. **Mauritania: Nouakchott** 34. Mauritius: Port Louis 35. **Morocco: Rabat** 36. Mozambique: Maputo 37. **Namibia: Windhoek** 38. Niger: Niamey 39. **Nigeria: Abuja** 40. Rwanda: Kigali 41. **Sao Tome and Principe: Sao Tome** 42. Senegal: Dakar 43. **Seychelles: Victoria** 44. Sierra Leone: Freetown 45. **Somalia: Mogadishu** 46. South Africa: Pretoria, Cape Town and Bloemfontein 47. **South Sudan: Juba** 48. Sudan: Khartoum 49. **Tanzania: Dodoma** 50. Togo: Lome 51. **Tunisia: Tunis** 52. Uganda: Kampala 53. **Zambia: Lusaka** 54. Zimbabwe: Harare

5 Kinds of Rhinos

There are only five kinds of rhinos in the world today, and they are all endangered. Black and white rhinos live in Africa, Sumatran rhinos live in Indonesia and Malaysia, Javan rhinos live in Malaysia, and greater one-horned rhinos live in India and Nepal. The Sumatran rhino has lived on Earth for longer than any other type of mammal.

1. **Sumatran rhinoceros**
2. Javan rhinoceros
3. **Black rhinoceros**
4. Greater one-horned rhinoceros
5. **White rhinoceros**

3 HORNED DINOSAURS

1. Triceratops is the most famous, with three huge horns on its head.

2. Kosmoceratops, a cousin of Triceratops, had 15 horns!

3. Styracosaurus had enormous spikes sticking out from its neck frill, as well as horns.

7 ANCIENT CITIES

◆ ◆ ◆

1. JERICHO, in the Middle East, established around 9,000 years ago.

2. ATHENS, Greece, established around 6,000 years ago.

3. UR, in modern-day Iraq, established around 5,800 years ago.

4. BABYLON, in modern-day Iraq, established around 5,300 years ago.

5. THEBES, now known as Luxor, in Egypt, established around 5,200 years ago.

6. MOHENDRO-DARO, in modern-day Pakistan, established around 4,500 years ago.

7. KNOSSOS, on Crete in Greece, established around 4,000 years ago.

10 ANIMALS with Interesting Names

• • • • • • • • • • • • •

1. WHITE-BELLIED GO-AWAY BIRD (Corythaixoides leucogaster)

2. PINK FAIRY ARMADILLO (Chlamyphorus truncates)

3. SCREAMING HAIRY ARMADILLO (Chaetophractus vellerosus)

4. BLOBFISH (Psychrolutes marcidus)

5. TERRIBLE HAIRY FLY (Mormotomyia hirsuta)

6. YELLOW-BELLIED SAPSUCKER (Sphyrapicus varius)

7. STAR-NOSED MOLE (Condylura cristata)

8. DUMBO OCTOPUS (Grimpoteuthis species)

9. YETI CRAB (Kiwa hirsuta)

10. RASPBERRY CRAZY ANT (Nylanderia fulva)

8 Jokes About Pirates

1. What did the pirate say when his peg leg got stuck in Arctic ice?
"Shiver me timbers!"

2. What do you call a pirate's lost parrot?
A polygon.

3. Why did the pirate tie a belt around a pumpkin?
He was a squash-buckler.

4. Knock, knock.
Who's there?
The interrupting pirate.
The interrupting pir—
Arrr!

5. What has eight eyes and eight legs?
Eight pirates.

6. Which pirate told the most jokes?
Captain Kidd.

7. What happened when pirates attacked a ship carrying blue and red paint?
The crew was marooned.

8. What marks did the pirate get in her exams?
High Cs.

17 US Presidents and Their Pets

Most presidents of the US have kept pets in the White House. Some had lots of pets, and some pets became almost as famous as the president. Here are some of the most numerous and/or interesting.

1. George Washington:
At least 8 dogs, 7 horses, a donkey, and a parrot called Snipe.

2. Thomas Jefferson:
Several mockingbirds, two dogs, three horses, and two grizzly bear cubs.

3. John Quincy Adams:
An alligator.

4. Andrew Jackson:
A parrot called Polly that swore, and several horses.

5. James Buchanan:
Two dogs and an eagle.

6. Abraham Lincoln:
Two goats, a turkey (saved from being Christmas dinner), several dogs, horses, cats, and a rabbit.

7. Rutherford B. Hayes:
Eight dogs and several cats, including the first Siamese cats in the US.

8. Benjamin Harrison:
Two opossums, a goat, and a dog.

9. William McKinley:
A Yellow-headed Mexican Parrot that could whistle Yankee Doodle and two Angora cats.

10. Theodore Roosevelt:
More than 30 pets, including ponies, lots of dogs, guinea pigs, cats, an owl, a badger, a laughing hyena, a Hyacinth Macaw, and a pig.

11. Woodrow Wilson:
Two dogs, a cat, songbirds, and sheep for mowing the White House lawn.

12. Calvin Coolidge:
Dozens of pets including 12 dogs, 13 ducks, a donkey, a raccoon, a pygmy hippo, and a wallaby.

13. Herbert Hoover:
Nine dogs and two alligators.

14. John F. Kennedy:
More than 20, including hamsters, dogs, ponies, parakeets, and a rabbit.

15. Lyndon B. Johnson:
Hamsters, lovebirds, and 6 dogs.

16. Bill Clinton:
Socks the cat became famous but eventually left the White House due to issues with the Clintons' other pet, Buddy the dog.

17. Barack Obama:
Portuguese water dogs called Bo and Sunny.

The MILKY WAY in 4 DIFFERENT LANGUAGES

. . . .

If you look up into the sky on a clear, moonless night, you can sometimes see a side-on view of our galaxy—the billions of stars make it look like a band of milky light. The Ancient Romans called it the Via Lactea—Milky Road or Milky Way. Here are some other countries' names for our galaxy:

1. PATH OF THE BIRDS —Finland

2. THE STRAW THIEF'S WAY —Armenia

3. THE WINTER WAY —Iceland

4. SILVER RIVER —China and other countries in Asia

6 Facts About Bats

. . . .

1. **There are more than 1,200 species of bats, which are the world's only flying mammals.**

2. Most bats feed on insects, but there are kinds that feed on fruit, nectar, small animals, fish, and blood.

3. **There are three kinds of blood-drinking vampire bats. Vampire bats find a big animal, such as a cow or a donkey, make a small cut in the skin, and lap up the blood.**

4. The smallest type of bat is the bumblebee bat, which is 1 $\frac{1}{2}$ in (4cm) long. It's also the world's smallest mammal.

5. **The biggest bat is the large flying fox, a type of fruit bat, which has a wingspan of nearly 6 ft (1.8m).**

6. Bats are active at night. Although all bats can see, most use echolocation to find their way around—they make noises and figure out their surroundings by how quickly the sound waves bounce back.

Unusual Phobias

1. **BUFONOPHOBIA: fear of toads**
2. Xanthophobia: fear of the color yellow
3. **Ombrophobia: fear of rain**
4. Pogonophobia: fear of beards
5. **COULROPHOBIA: fear of clowns**
6. Pupaphobia: fear of puppets
7. **Turophobia: fear of cheese**
8. Nomophobia: fear of being without a working mobile phone
9. **PAPAPHOBIA: fear of the pope**
10. Alektorophobia: fear of chickens
11. **Genuphobia: fear of knees**
12. Lutraphobia: fear of otters
13. **OMPHALOPHOBIA: fear of the navel**
14. Pediophobia: fear of dolls
15. **Linonophobia: fear of string**
16. Blennophobia: fear of slime
17. **CHOROPHOBIA: fear of dancing**
18. Brontophobia: fear of thunder and lightning
19. **Trypophobia: fear of holes**
20. Kathisophobia: fear of sitting down
21. **PLACOPHOBIA: Fear of tombstones**
22. Isopterophobia: fear of insects that eat wood

8 LOST CIVILIZATIONS

1. **Sumer, Middle East, 5000–2000 BCE**

2. Indus Valley civilization, India and Pakistan, 5500–1500 BCE

3. **Minoan, Greece, 2700–1500 BCE**

4. Nok, Nigeria, 1000 BCE–500 CE

5. **Maya, Central America, 2600 BCE–900 CE**

6. Anasazi, North America, 1200s–1500s CE

7. **Inca, South America, 1200s–1500s CE**

8. Rapa Nui, South Pacific, 300s–1800s CE

5 EMPIRES that Lasted the Longest

1. **Maya, Central America: 3,540 years**

2. Chinese: 2,133 years

3. **Chola, India, and South Asia: 1,579 years**

4. Pandyan, India: 1,300 years

5. **Roman, Europe, North Africa, and Near East: 1,119 years**

6 DANGEROUS ROADS

If you're worried about rockslides, stomach-churning cliff edges, or vast, hostile landscapes miles from help, steer clear of these roads.

1. **North Yungas Road, Bolivia**

Also known as the Road of Death, this highway winds along a mountainside with terrifying drops.

2. **James Dalton Highway, Alaska, US**

The winds that scour the desolate, frozen landscape here can carry rocks.

3. **California State Route 138, US**

Clinging to the side of the San Bernardino Mountains, this winding road makes passing perilous.

4. **Karakoram Highway, Pakistan to China**

This road is the highest paved road in the world, more than nearly 3 miles (4,700m) high up in the Karakoram mountains. Dangers include landslides and avalanches.

5. **Eyre Highway, Australia**

This straight, flat road cuts across a desert, one of the most hostile environments on Earth.

6. **Zoji Pass, India**

This road zigzags through the Himalayan mountain range. Watch out for steep drops and rockslides.

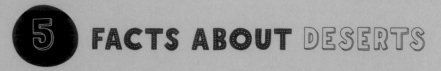

5 FACTS ABOUT DESERTS

1. About a third of all the land on Earth is desert.

2. All deserts are dry—there is very little rainfall. But not all of them are hot—the Antarctic is the world's biggest desert, with less than 9 in (200mm) of rainfall per year at the coast and even less inland. It's also the coldest place on Earth, with temperatures as low as -129°F (-89.2°C). The Arctic is also a desert.

3. The Mojave Desert, spanning California, Nevada, and Utah, includes one of the most famously hot and dangerous places in the world—Death Valley. The temperature there can reach 129°F (54°C).

4. Badain Jaran Desert in China has the world's biggest sand dunes—some are 1,600 ft (500m) tall.

5. The Atacama Desert in Chile is the driest place in the world after Antarctica. Rainfall has never been recorded in some parts of the desert.

The World's
6 Biggest Deserts

1. **Antarctic—5.4 million mi² (14 million km²)**
2. Arctic—6.4 million mi² (13.985 million km²)
3. **Sahara—3.5 million mi² (9 million km²)**
4. Australian—1 million mi² (2.7 million km²)
5. **Arabian—9 million mi² (2.33 million km²)**
6. Gobi—500,000 mi² (1.3 million km²)

3 Animals with Far Too Many Legs

These centipedes and a millipede have way more than their fair share of legs. In case you were wondering about the differences between them, millipedes have two pairs of legs per body segment, while centipedes have one, and centipedes catch and kill other creatures to eat, while millipedes eat plants.

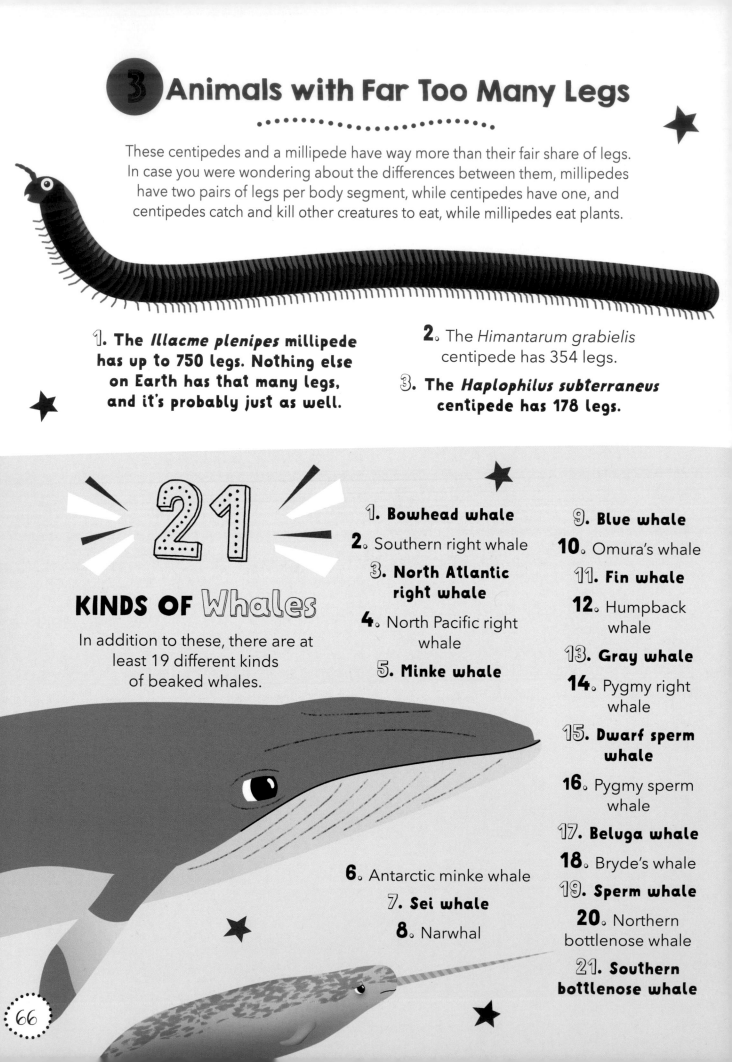

1. The *Illacme plenipes* millipede has up to 750 legs. Nothing else on Earth has that many legs, and it's probably just as well.

2. The *Himantarum grabielis* centipede has 354 legs.

3. The *Haplophilus subterraneus* centipede has 178 legs.

21 KINDS OF Whales

In addition to these, there are at least 19 different kinds of beaked whales.

1. Bowhead whale
2. Southern right whale
3. **North Atlantic right whale**
4. North Pacific right whale
5. **Minke whale**
6. Antarctic minke whale
7. **Sei whale**
8. Narwhal
9. Blue whale
10. Omura's whale
11. **Fin whale**
12. Humpback whale
13. **Gray whale**
14. Pygmy right whale
15. **Dwarf sperm whale**
16. Pygmy sperm whale
17. **Beluga whale**
18. Bryde's whale
19. **Sperm whale**
20. Northern bottlenose whale
21. **Southern bottlenose whale**

5 Fearless Female Warriors

1. Tomyris, **Queen of the Massagetae, who defeated Persian leader Cyrus the Great in the 500s BCE.**

2. **Boudicca**, Queen of the Iceni people in Britain, who led an army against the Romans in 61 CE.

3. Queen Zenobia of Palmyra, **who fought the Romans in the 200s CE.**

4. Samurai warrior **Tomoe Gozen**, who fought in the Gempei War in Japan in the 1100s.

5. Joan of Arc, **the teenage farm girl who led the French army in the 1400s.**

8 ANIMAL MUMMIES

The following animals were all made into mummies by the Ancient Egyptians.

1. **Cats** 2. Crocodiles
3. **Ibises** 4. Baboons 5. **Fish**
6. Snakes 7. **Dogs** 8. Jackals

14 Formula One Grand Prix Winners*

1. **Lewis Hamilton (UK)**
103 Grand Prix wins.

2. Michael Schumacher (Germany)
91 Grand Prix wins.

3. **Sebastian Vettel (Germany)**
53 Grand Prix wins.

4. Alain Prost (France)
51 Grand Prix wins.

5. **Ayrton Senna (Brazil)**
41 Grand Prix wins.

6. Fernando Alonso (Spain)
32 Grand Prix wins.

7. **Nigel Mansell (UK)**
31 Grand Prix wins.

8. Jackie Stewart (UK)
27 Grand Prix wins.

9. **Jim Clark (UK)**
25 Grand Prix wins.

10. Niki Lauda (Austria)
25 Grand Prix wins.

11. **Juan Manuel Fangio (Argentina)**
24 Grand Prix wins.

12. Nelson Piquet (Brazil)
23 Grand Prix wins.

13. **Nico Rosberg (Germany)**
23 Grand Prix wins.

14. Damon Hill (UK)
22 Grand Prix wins.

* as of Dec 2021

88 Constellations

The Ancient Sumerians were the first people to group stars together and give them names. Later, the Greeks and Romans, and later still people from Europe and the Americas, named constellations. Some are named after characters from mythology, some are named after animals, and some are named after objects, such as the Air Pump! Here are the 88 constellations that are recognized today.

1. Andromeda—princess from Greek mythology
2. Antlia—air pump
3. Apus—bird-of-paradise
4. Aquarius—water carrier
5. Aquila—eagle
6. Ara—altar
7. Aries—ram
8. Auriga—charioteer
9. Boötes—herdsman
10. Caelum—chisel
11. Camelopardalis—giraffe
12. Cancer—crab
13. Canes Venatici—hunting dogs
14. Canis Major—great dog
15. Canis Minor—small dog
16. Capricornus—goat
17. Carina—keel (of a ship)
18. Cassiopeia—queen from Greek mythology
19. Centaurus—half-human half-horse from Greek mythology

20. Cepheus—king from Greek mythology
21. Cetus—sea monster/whale
22. Chamaeleon—chameleon
23. Circinus—compasses
24. Columba—dove
25. Coma Berenices—Berenice's (queen of Cyrene and Egypt) hair
26. Corona Australis—southern crown
27. Corona Borealis—northern crown
28. Corvus—crow
29. Crater—cup
30. Crux—southern cross
31. Cygnus—swan (also known as the northern cross)
32. Delphinus—dolphin
33. Dorado—dolphinfish
34. Draco—dragon
35. Equuleus—pony
36. Eridanus—river in Greek mythology
37. Fornax—furnace
38. Gemini—twins

39. Grus–crane (bird)

40. Hercules–hero from Greek mythology

41. Horologium–pendulum clock

42. Hydra–water monster from Greek mythology

43. Hydrus–water snake

44. Indus–Indian

45. Lacerta–lizard

46. Leo–lion

47. Leo Minor–small lion

48. Lepus–hare

49. Libra–scales

50. Lupus–wolf

51. Lynx–lynx

52. Lyra–harp

53. Mensa–Table Mountain (in South Africa)

54. Microscopium–microscope

55. Monoceros–unicorn

56. Musca–fly

57. Norma–spirit level

58. Octans–octant (navigational instrument)

59. Ophiuchus –serpent bearer

60. Orion–huntsman from Greek mythology

61. Pavo–peacock

62. Pegasus–flying horse from Greek mythology

63. Perseus–hero from Greek mythology

64. Phoenix–phoenix (mythological bird)

65. Pictor–easel

66. Pisces–fish

67. Piscis Austrinus–southern fish

68. Puppis–poop deck (on a ship)

69. Pyxis–mariner's compass

70. Reticulum–sight-markings in an eyepiece

71. Sagitta–arrow

72. Sagittarius–archer

73. Scorpius–scorpion

74. Sculptor–sculptor

75. Scutum–shield

76. Serpens–snake

77. Sextans–sextant (navigational instrument)

78. Taurus–bull

79. Telescopium–telescope

80. Triangulum–triangle

81. Triangulum Australe - southern triangle

82. Tucana–toucan

83. Ursa Major–great bear

84. Ursa Minor–small bear

85. Vela–sails

86. Virgo–virgin

87. Volans–flying fish

88. Vulpecula–fox

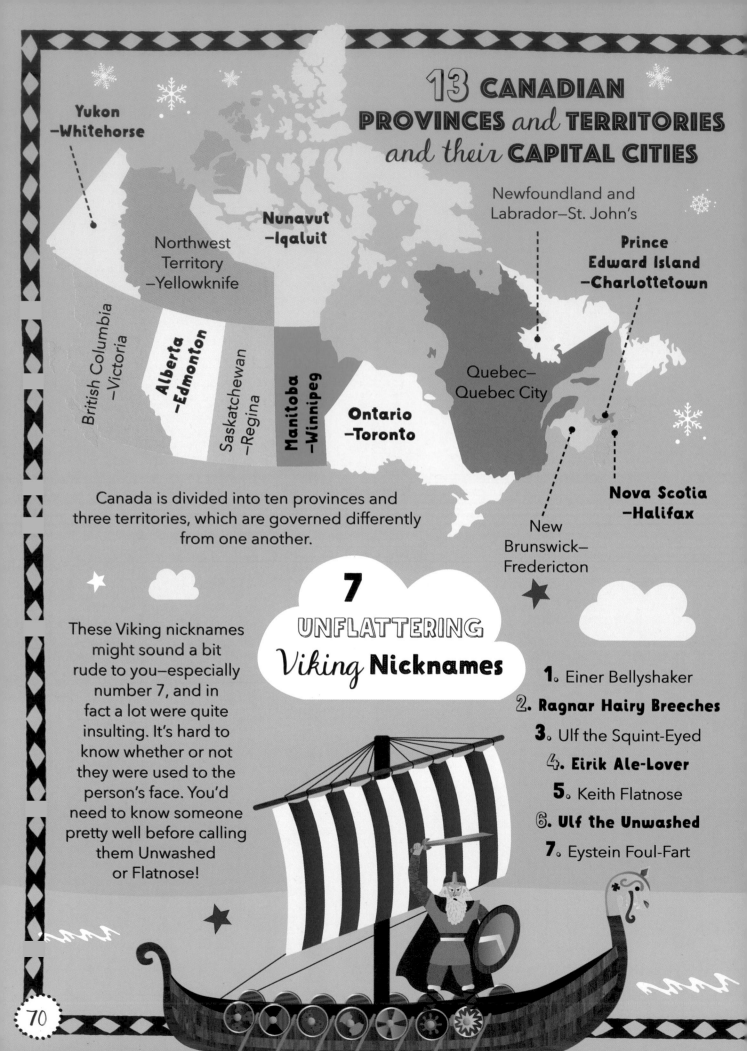

13 CANADIAN PROVINCES and TERRITORIES and their CAPITAL CITIES

Yukon
–Whitehorse

Northwest Territory
–Yellowknife

Nunavut
–Iqaluit

Newfoundland and Labrador—St. John's

Prince Edward Island
–Charlottetown

British Columbia
–Victoria

Alberta
–Edmonton

Saskatchewan
–Regina

Manitoba
–Winnipeg

Ontario
–Toronto

Quebec—
Quebec City

New Brunswick—
Fredericton

Nova Scotia
–Halifax

Canada is divided into ten provinces and three territories, which are governed differently from one another.

7 UNFLATTERING Viking Nicknames

These Viking nicknames might sound a bit rude to you—especially number 7, and in fact a lot were quite insulting. It's hard to know whether or not they were used to the person's face. You'd need to know someone pretty well before calling them Unwashed or Flatnose!

1. Einer Bellyshaker
2. Ragnar Hairy Breeches
3. Ulf the Squint-Eyed
4. Eirik Ale-Lover
5. Keith Flatnose
6. Ulf the Unwashed
7. Eystein Foul-Fart

8 ALTERNATIVES to Plastic

1. **Bioplastics are made from plants, which are broken down to form polylactic acid (PLA). PLA can be used to make plastic wrap and food containers.**

2. Chitin is a natural plastic made from shrimp and crab shells, and can be made into chitosan, used in food and other packaging.

3. **Bagasse, a by-product of the sugarcane industry, can be molded into packaging.**

4. Mycelium, a kind of mushroom root that Quorn is made from, can also be made into packaging.

5. **Wood pulp can be made into a film similar to cellophane.**

6. Palm leaves from the areca palm can be used to package food and other products.

7. **Milk protein called casein can be used to make plastic that's used for detergent packaging.**

8. Corn starch can be made into little chips to be used instead of polystyrene.

15 POISONOUS GARDEN *Plants*

1. **Oleander (Nerium oleander)**

2. Foxglove (Digitalis purpurea)

3. **Monkshood (Aconitum)**

4. Rhododendron (Rhododendron ponticum)

5. **Lily of the valley (Convallaria majalis)**

6. Larkspur (Delphinium consolida)

7. **Water hemlock (Cicuta maculata)**

8. Passionflower (Passiflora caerulea)

9. **Deadly nightshade (Atropa belladonna)**

10. Hydrangea (Hydrangea macrophylla)

11. **Poinsettia (Euphorbia pulcherrima)**

12. Snowdrop (Galanthus nivalis)

13. **Ivy (Hedera helix)**

14. Lily (Lilium)

15. **Daffodil (Narcissus)**

6 Egyptian
FACTS

1. Ancient Egyptians made dead people into mummies by removing some of their insides, embalming them, then wrapping the bodies in bandages. The bandages on just one mummy could be nearly a mile (1.5km) long.

2. Pyramids were built as tombs for Egyptian pharaohs (rulers). Later pharaohs built tombs in the Valley of the Kings instead of inside pyramids.

3. The heart was very important to Ancient Egyptians, so when someone died their heart was given special treatment. The Egyptians didn't think the brain was important at all—they removed it from a dead body and threw it away.

4. There were more than 700 hieroglyphs in the Ancient Egyptian alphabet. Only scribes could read them—most people in Ancient Egypt couldn't read and write.

5. Cats were special to the Ancient Egyptians and often kept as pets for good luck. There was a cat goddess called Bastet, and harsh punishments for anyone who hurt a cat.

6. The Ancient Egyptians used toothpaste. One recipe included salt, pepper, mint, and dried flowers, which doesn't sound too bad. Another one included ox hooves, which does.

12 Ancient Greek and Roman Gods

These were the most important gods for the Ancient Greeks. The Romans worshipped some of the same gods as the Greeks, but gave them different names.

GREEK NAME	ROMAN NAME	JOB
Zeus	Jupiter	chief god
Hera	Juno	chief goddess
Hermes	Mercury	messenger god
Aphrodite	Venus	goddess of love
Poseidon	Neptune	god of the sea
Apollo	Apollo	god of the sun, music, and healing
Hephaestos	Vulcan	god of volcanoes and metalworking
Ares	Mars	god of war
Hades	Pluto	god of the underworld
Dionysus	Bacchus	god of wine
Artemis	Diana	the hunter goddess
Athena	Minerva	goddess of wisdom

29 Flowers and Their Symbolisms

In days gone by, a bunch of flowers could mean much more than it does today. To be on the safe side, consult this list before giving flowers to anyone!

1. Aster—love, daintiness
2. **Begonia—beware!**
3. Bluebell—humility, kindness
4. **Candytuft—indifference**
5. Carnation (red)—admiration
6. **Carnation (white)—pure love**
7. Carnation (yellow)—rejection

5 Unusual ANCIENT ROMAN GODDESSES

1. Cardea, goddess of door hinges

2. Bubona, goddess of cattle

3. Cloacina, goddess of sewers

4. Devera, goddess of brooms used to purify temples

5. Mellona, goddess of bees

6 Animals That Live Only in Caves

These are a few of the many creatures that spend their whole lives in the dark. Although mammals often shelter in caves, there are none that live only in caves—bats sleep in caves but come out to hunt.

1. Cave crayfish—white in color and completely blind.

2. Kaua'i cave wolf spider—found only in a few caves in the Kaua'i region of Hawaii, this spider has no eyes at all.

3. Cave rat snake—this snake lives in caves in Mexico, where it dangles from the cave ceiling to snatch passing bats.

4. Olm—a blind white salamander that lives in caves in southeastern Europe.

5. Blind cave eel—a colorless fish that lives in caves in western Australia.

6. Tumbling Creek cave snail—this water snail glows in the dark! It lives only in the Tumbling Creek caves in Missouri, US.

8. Carnation (pink) —I'll never forget you

9. Chrysanthemum —cheerfulness

10. Daffodil—regard

11. Daisy—innocence

12. Forget-me-not— memories of true love

13. Gardenia—secret love

14. Iris—a message

15. Jasmine—sweet love

16. Lavender—devotion

17. Lilac—joy of youth

18. Calla lily—beauty

19. Poppy—consolation

20. Rose (red)—I love you

21. Rose (pink)—happiness

22. Rose (yellow)—jealousy

23. Rose (white)—purity

24. Sunflower—adoration

25. Sweet pea—pleasure

26. Tulip (red) —I love you

27. Tulip (yellow) —sunshine in your smile

28. Violet—loyalty

29. Willow—sadness

33 SUMMER OLYMPIC GAMES
Host Cities

The modern Olympic Games began in 1896. Since then, the Games have been held every four years, apart from in 1916, due to the First World War, and in 1940 and 1944, due to the Second World War.

1. Athens, Greece 1896
2. **Paris, France 1900**
3. St. Louis, US 1904
4. **London, UK 1908**
5. Stockholm, Sweden 1912
6. **Antwerp, Belgium 1920**
7. Paris, France 1924
8. **Amsterdam, Netherlands 1928**
9. Los Angeles, US 1932
10. **Berlin, Germany 1936**
11. London, UK 1948
12. **Helsinki, Finland 1952**
13 and 14. Melbourne, Australia, and Stockholm, Sweden 1956
15. **Rome, Italy 1960**
16. Tokyo, Japan 1964
17. **Mexico City, Mexico 1968**
18. Munich, West Germany 1972
19. **Montreal, Canada 1976**
20. Moscow, Soviet Union 1980
21. **Los Angeles, US 1984**
22. Seoul, South Korea 1988
23. **Barcelona, Spain 1992**
24. Atlanta, US 1996
25. **Sydney, Australia 2000**
26. Athens, Greece 2004
27. **Beijing, China 2008**
28. London, UK 2012
29. **Rio de Janeiro, Brazil 2016**
30. Tokyo, Japan 2020
31. **Paris, France 2024**
32. Los Angeles, US 2028
33. **Brisbane, Australia 2032**

3 Super-Fast RUNNERS

These sprinters have made the fastest times in the world over 100 m.

1. Usain Bolt (Jamaica)
Fastest Time: 9.58 seconds

2. **Tyson Gay (US)**
Fastest Time: 9.69 seconds

3. Yohan Blake (Jamaica)
Fastest Time: 9.69 seconds

18 Animal Astronauts

Fruit flies were the first living things to be sent into space from Earth, in 1947. Since then all sorts of creatures have become space travelers.

1. Fruit flies
2. **Mice**
3. Chimpanzee (called Ham)
4. **Dogs (including Laika, Strelka, Belka, Tsygan, and Desik)**
5. Orb-weaver spiders (called Arabella and Anita)
6. **Bullfrogs**
7. Honey bees (which built a hive on their trip)
8. **Wasps**
9. Rats
10. **Tortoises (which hold the record for the longest animal space flight)**
11. Guinea pigs
12. **Cats**
13. Cockroaches
14. **Jellyfish**
15. Snails
16. **Scorpions**
17. Newts
18. **Silkworms**

12 Chinese Zodiac Animals

1. **Rat** 2. Ox 3. **Tiger** 4. Rabbit
5. **Dragon** 6. Snake 7. **Horse**
8. Sheep 9. **Monkey** 10. Rooster
11. **Dog** 12. Pig

4 Enormous Rodents

1. **The capybara, from South America, is the biggest rodent in the world today. It looks like a giant guinea pig, measures up to 53 in (134cm) long, and weighs more than you do–up to 146 lb (66kg)!**

2. Nutrias, or coypu, can weigh up to 37 lb (17kg). They're originally from South America, but their giant teeth helped them escape from fur farms all over the world, and they're now widespread.

3. **Beavers are the next biggest rodent. They can be 47 in (120cm) long and weigh up to 66 lb (30kg). They live in forests in North America, Europe, and Asia.**

4. None of these modern-day rodents is anywhere near as big as the largest one of all time (as far as we know): the giant pacarana, which weighed up to a ton. It died out around two million years ago.

The Beaufort Scale

The Beaufort Scale measures wind. It's divided into values from 0 (calm) to 12 (hurricanes).

0. CALM
The sea is smooth and smoke from a fire rises straight up.

1. LIGHT AIR
Winds of 1–3 mph (3–6km/h). Smoke shows the direction the wind is blowing.

2. SLIGHT BREEZE
Winds of 4–7mph (7–11km/h). Wind rustles leaves in the trees.

3. GENTLE BREEZE
Winds of 8–11 mph (12–19km/h). Makes a flag extend.

4. MODERATE BREEZE
Winds of 12–18 mph (20–28km/h). Causes white caps on waves at sea.

5. FRESH BREEZE
Winds of 19–24 mph (29–38km/h). Makes trees sway.

6. STRONG BREEZE
Winds of 25–31 mph (39km/h). Causes waves on the surface of the sea.

7. NEAR GALE
Winds of 32–38 mph (50–61km/h). Large trees sway.

8. GALE
Winds of 39–45 mph (67–74 km/h). High seas, twigs break from branches.

9. STRONG GALE
Winds of 46–54 mph (75–88km/h). Branches break off trees.

10. STORM
Winds of 55–63 mph (89–102km/h). Uproots trees.

11. STRONG STORM
Winds of 64–135 mph (103–117km/h). Widespread damage.

12. HURRICANE
Winds of more than 136 mph (118km/h). Severe damage to buildings, trees, etc.

5 Facts About Sloths

1. Sloths spend 90 percent of their time hanging around in trees. Contrary to popular belief, in the wild many sloths only sleep for about the same amount of time you do—up to about 10 hours. In captivity, they spend longer asleep.

2. Their long claws make it difficult for sloths to move about on land—they crawl along at only 12 in (30cm) a minute.

3. Sloths come down from their trees about once a week to poop.

4. Sloths often grow algae on their fur, which makes them appear green in color and helps camouflage them in the trees.

5. Modern-day sloths are quite small—about the size of an average dog. But 10,000 years ago, a massive sloth called *Megatherium* lumbered about on the ground in South America. It was the size of an elephant, and much too big to live in trees.

THE WORLD'S 5 Highest Mountains

The Himalaya mountain range really is very high indeed. All five of the world's highest peaks are in the Himalayas.

1. MOUNT EVEREST
Height: 829,029 ft (8,848m)

2. K2
Height: 28,251 ft (8,611m)

3. KANGCHENJUNGA
Height: 28,169 ft (8,586m)

4. LHOTSE
Height: 27,940 ft (8,516m)

5. MAKALU
Height: 27,766 ft (8,463m)

4 Fruity Facts

1. Strawberries are the only fruit to have seeds on the outside.

2. There are around 1,000 different varieties of banana plants, but almost all of them don't taste very good. The banana that's widely eaten is a single variety called the Cavendish.

3. The seeds and pits of lots of different kinds of fruit contain the poison cyanide. The fruits with the most cyanide in their pits are greengages and apricots.

4. The heaviest watermelon ever recorded weighed 351 lb (159kg).

11 Incredibly Fast Roller Coasters

These roller coasters are not for the faint-hearted. They whizz along at stomach-churning speeds.

1. **Formula Rossa, Ferrari World, United Arab Emirates: 150 mph (241.4km/h)**

2. Kingda Ka, Six Flags Great Adventure, New Jersey: 128 mph (206km/h)

3. **Top Thrill Dragster, Cedar Point, Ohio: 120 mph (193.1km/h)**

4. Red Force Vertical Accelerator, Ferrari Land, Salou, Spain: 112 mph (180km/h)

5. **Dodonpa, Fuji-Q Highland Amusement Park, Yamanashi, Japan: 107 mph (172.2km/h)**

6. Superman: Escape from Krypton, Six Flags Magic Mountain Park, California: 100 mph (160.9km/h)

7. **Ring Racer, Nürburgring Motor Sports Complex, Germany: 99 mph (160km/h)**

8. Steel Dragon 2000, Nagashima Spa Land Amusement Park, Mie Prefecture, Japan: 95 mph (152.9km/h)

9. **Millennium Force, Cedar Point, Ohio: 93 mph (149.7km/h)**

10. Leviathan, Canada's Wonderland, Ontario, Canada: 92 mph (148km/h)

11. **Intimidator 305, Kings Dominion Park, Virginia: 90 mph (145km/h)**

10 Monsters from Ancient Greek Mythology

1. The Gorgons: three snake-haired women called Stheno, Euryale, and Medusa, whose stare turns people to stone.

2. The Graeae: three very old women, sisters of the Gorgons, who share one eye and one tooth among the three of them.

5. Sirens: winged women whose beautiful song lures sailors to a horrible death.

6. The Echidna: part woman, part snake, the Echidna is the mother of Cerberus, the Hydra, the Chimera, the Sphinx, and the Nemean Lion.

7. The Hydra: swamp-dwelling nine-headed water monster.

8. Cerberus: the three-headed dog that guards the entrance to the Underworld.

3. Satyrs: part man, part goat with the tail of a horse, satyrs are fun-loving friends of the wine god, Dionysus.

4. Centaurs: part man, part horse, centaurs are also friends of Dionysus and famous for their wild and violent behavior.

9. The Chimera: with a goat's head, a lion's body, and a snake for a tail, the Chimera terrorizes the people of Lycia.

10. Harpies: with birds' bodies and the faces of old women, harpies carry victims off to the Underworld.

7 AMAZON RAIN FOREST FACTS

· · · · · · · · · · · · · · · · · · · ·

1. The Amazon rain forest is the biggest rain forest in the world, and also the oldest. It may have existed at the time of the dinosaurs.

2. The Amazon stretches across nine countries: Brazil, Bolivia, Peru, Colombia, Ecuador, Guyana, Suriname, Venezuela, and French Guiana.

3. There are about a million native Amazonians who live in the rain forest, some of whom have contact with the outside world, and some of whom remain uncontacted. Each of the 400 or so tribes has its own language and culture.

4. Rain forests are like the Earth's lungs —they recycle carbon dioxide into oxygen. The planet would die without them.

5. The Amazon rain forest is home to millions of different plant and animal species—2.5 million different types of insects, 40,000 different plant species, 3,000 different types of fishes, 1,300 bird species, and 400 different species each of reptile, mammal, and amphibian.

6. The thousands of different plant species of the Amazon have been used to make medicines, including drugs that help people with cancer.

7. Sadly, an area of the Amazon rain forest the size of England is destroyed every year. The trees are felled and used for lumber, and farms are created to take their place.

5 Facts About Hot-Air Balloons

Not for the faint-hearted, the first glass-bottomed hot-air balloon made its first voyage in 2010.

The hot-air balloon was invented by the Montgolfier brothers in France. Its first flight was in 1783, with three passengers onboard: a sheep called Montauciel, a duck, and a rooster. All of them came back safely.

1.

Hot-air balloons were used to observe the enemy in the American Civil War and the French Revolution.

4.

After the animals' successful flight, two human passengers took a balloon trip and became the first people to fly.

3.

2.

The world's biggest hot-air balloon festival is the Albuquerque International Balloon Fiesta, which takes place every year in New Mexico, US, and involves hundreds of balloons.

5.

3 MARATHON SWIMS

1. **The English Channel** (between England and France)—21 mi (34km).

2. The Cook Strait (between New Zealand's North and South Islands) —14 mi (22km), known for strong currents.

3. **The Catalina Channel** (between California and Santa Catalina Island) —20 mi (32.5km), known for sharks and jellyfish.

7 Unusual *Festivals*

1. BORYEONG MUD FESTIVAL,
South Korea
Attractions include mud pools, mud body-painting, and mud skiing competitions.

2. LA TOMATINA, Buñol, Spain
A massive tomato fight takes place in the town of Buñol every August.

3. MONKEY BUFFET FESTIVAL,
Lopburi, Thailand
An enormous buffet is laid out for the local monkey population to enjoy.

4. BATTLE OF THE ORANGES,
Ivrea, Italy
Nine teams pelt one another with oranges in a huge food fight.

5. UP HELLY AA, Shetland,
Scotland, UK
Every January in the town of Lerwick, locals set fire to a large boat that they've constructed over the previous year.

6. SONGKRAN FESTIVAL,
Thailand
All over Thailand people take part in the world's biggest water-pistol fight to celebrate the New Year.

7. UNDERWATER MUSIC FESTIVAL,
Looe Key Reef, Florida, US
People play underwater instruments and wear costumes.

10 Norse Gods

There are dozens of gods and goddesses in Norse mythology. These are some of the most important.

1. **Odin, chief god**

2. Frigga, chief goddess

3. **Thor, thunderbolt-carrying god of the sky**

4. Brag, god of poetry

5. **Hel, god of the dead**

6. Skadi, goddess of winter and hunting

7. **Loki, shape-changing trickster god**

8. Aegir, god of the sea

9. **Tyr, god of war**

10. Freyja, goddess of love

5
Expensive cars

If you have several million dollars handy, you might be in the market for one of these:
1. Zenvo STI
2. Ferrari F-60 America
3. Pagani Huayra
4. Aston Martin One-77
5. Koenigsegg CCXR Trevita

5
HISTORICAL
STATUS SYMBOLS

People have always liked to show off, but status symbols in the past were very different from today's posh cars and clothes.

1. Pineapples
became a symbol of luxury
in Europe in the 1600s and 1700s because
only the rich could afford them. A single
fruit could cost the equivalent of thousands
of dollars today. Instead of being eaten, pineapples
were put on display—sometimes for months!

2. Pointed shoes—known as poulaines—were a symbol of wealth in the Middle Ages. The points were stuffed with wool, moss, hair, or grass, and could be as long as 24 inches (60cm)! Laws limited the length of the toes by social class, so that only the highest-ranking people could wear the longest-toed shoes.

3. In the Netherlands in the 1600s, beautiful, colorful
tulips were introduced from Turkey and quickly became a
status symbol. The flowers became so highly prized that tulip
bulbs were bought and sold for huge sums of money—a single
bulb could cost ten times an artisan's yearly wage.

4. If you were really posh in Britain in the 1700s, to go with your mansion you'd have a beautifully designed landscape garden, which included some kind of unusual building, and, preferably, a hermit to live in it.

5. Sugar used to be expensive and hard
to come by, and large, intricate sculptures,
called "subtleties," were displayed at
various times throughout history
to show off wealth.

7 Random World Records

1. Longest distance keeping a table lifted with teeth (the record is 39 ft (11.8m)–the table had a woman sitting on it).

2. Most canned drinks opened by a parrot in one minute (Zac the macaw opened 35).

3. Fastest mile on a pogo stick while juggling three balls (the record is 23 minutes 28 seconds).

4. Most apples held in own mouth and cut by chainsaw in one minute (the record is 28).

5. Largest knitting needles (14.5 ft (4.42m) long).

6. Fastest 100 m distance on a skateboard by a dog (Jumpy did it in 19.65 seconds).

7. Largest group of people dressed as cats (there were 440 of them).

7 Kinds of Sea Turtles

There are only seven species of sea turtles in the world.

1. LEATHERBACK
Leatherbacks are the biggest of all turtles, up to 8 ft (2.5m) long and up to 2,000 lb (900kg) in weight. They've lived on Earth for more than 150 million years!

2. LOGGERHEAD
Loggerhead turtles are the largest hard-shelled turtle and have a powerful jaw. They eat animals with hard shells, such as crabs and shellfish.

3. GREEN
Young green turtles eat anything, but when they grow up they become vegetarian.

4. HAWKSBILL
These turtles have beautiful patterned shells, and a narrow beak that they use to grab food—mostly sponges—from rock crevices.

5. FLATBACK
Flatback turtles are named for their flat shell. Unlike other turtles, they don't migrate. They live around the coasts of Northern Australia, Southern Indonesia, and Southern Papua New Guinea.

6. OLIVE RIDLEY
Olive Ridley turtles are the world's most common turtles, but they're still under threat.

7. KEMP'S RIDLEY
The smallest of the sea turtles, Kemp's Ridley turtles were on the brink of becoming extinct. They're doing much better now, but they're still at risk.

6 Facts About Bacteria

Bacteria are single-celled life forms. Life on Earth began with bacteria, and they're still around today, in vast quantities. Here are a few mind-boggling facts about bacteria.

1. **There are more bacteria in your body than there are human cells.**

2. There are more E. coli bacteria in one person's gut than the number of human beings who have ever lived—and that's just one type of bacteria. Without all the bacteria in our bodies, we wouldn't be alive.

3. **Scientists revived a bacterium that had been frozen in Antarctic ice for 8 million years.**

4. Bacteria can live inside volcanoes, boiling hydrothermal vents, and even in space.

5. **There are even bacteria that live on electricity! They're found on seabeds and riverbanks.**

6. One kind of bacteria lives in acidic caves, where they hang in slimy colonies from the cave ceiling like snotty stalactites. Scientists have named them snottites.

6 FACTS ABOUT THE HUMAN BRAIN

1. **The brain is the body's control center. It's more powerful than any computer in the world.**

2. The brain is made up of special cells called neurons, which connect with one another. There are around one hundred billion of them in the brain altogether.

3. **The brain's surface, the cerebral cortex, stores most of the brain's information and is how we sense things, think, and remember. It is wrinkled so it fits inside the skull, but if it were flattened it would measure about 400 in² (40cm²). You would need quite a big, flat head for that.**

4. There are around 10 billion brain cells in the cerebral cortex, and they make hundreds of thousands of connections all the time, which can change 200 times per second.

5. **When you're ten years old, your brain is the same size as it's going to be when you're an adult. On average, it weighs around 5 lb (2.25kg).**

6. A brain museum in Peru contains nearly 3,000 human brains. The biggest human brain collection in the world, with nearly 6,700 brains, is at Harvard Brain Tissue Resource Center, Belmont, Massachusetts, US.

4 FAMOUS BRAINS

1. The scientist **ALBERT EINSTEIN** is famous for his genius theories about relativity. After his death in 1955, and against his wishes, his brain was removed and studied, but there are no definite conclusions about it. The brain is now housed in Princeton University, US, where Einstein was a professor.

2. PAUL BROCA was a scientist who studied the part of the brain involved with language, which has been named "Broca's area" after him. He kept a large collection of brains, and his own was added to it when he died in 1880.

3. CHARLES BABBAGE, mathematician, engineer, and computer pioneer, donated his brain to science after he died in 1871. Half of it is in the Hunterian Museum and the other half in the Science Museum, both in London, UK.

4. VLADIMIR LENIN, one of the leaders of the Russian Revolution, died in 1924. His brain was removed and studied for signs of genius, and his body was mummified and put on display in Moscow, Russia.

★ 4 FACTS ABOUT HIPPOS ★

1. Hippos weigh 2.5 tons or more and measure 5 ft (1.5m) at the shoulder.

2. Hippos spend most of their time in water, but come onto land to eat grass. They can hold their breath for up to five minutes, and can breathe and see while mostly underwater because their eyes and nostrils are near the top of their heads.

3. Hippos can be very aggressive, especially if they're with their young or if their path to water is blocked. They have huge teeth up to 28 in (70cm) long and have been known to kill people.

4. Hippos like to mark their territory by twirling their tails as they poop, spreading the dung over as big an area as possible.

THE 12 Labors of HERACLES

In an Ancient Greek myth, heroic Heracles had to complete these 12 tricky tasks for King Eurystheus.

1. Kill the Nemean Lion
The lion's hide was weapon-proof, but Heracles killed the lion and used its skin as a cloak.

2. Kill the Lernaean Hydra
The hydra was a many-headed water monster. Every time Heracles chopped off one head, two new ones grew back.

3. Capture the Cerynean Hind
The hind was an enormous deer with golden antlers and bronze hooves. It took Heracles a year to capture it.

4. Capture the Erymanthian Boar
The boar was so monstrous that the king hid in a big jar when Heracles brought it to him.

5. Clean The Augean Stables
Heracles had to alter the course of a river to clean the stables.

6. Drive Away the Stymphalian Birds
The birds were bronze-beaked man-eaters with poisonous droppings, but Heracles got rid of them with arrows from the gods.

7. Capture the Cretan Bull
The bull was causing all sorts of destruction, but Heracles crept up on it and grabbed it by the horns.

8. Steal the Mares of King Diomedes
Naturally, these horses were man-eaters too.

9. Fetch the Girdle of the Queen of the Amazons
Hippolyte, fearsome Queen of the Amazons, was not well pleased.

10. Capture the Cattle of Geryon
Geryon was a three-bodied man with a vicious, two-headed dog. The cows were OK, however.

11. Fetch the Apples of the Hesperides
These golden apples were guarded by a dragon.

12. Bring Cerberus from the Underworld
Cerberus is the three-headed dog that guards the Underworld.

6 Facts About the *Amazon* River

1. The Amazon is the biggest river in the world by volume of water. There is fierce competition between the Amazon and the Nile for the longest river in the world.

2. The river starts in Peru in the Andes Mountains and flows across South America to the Atlantic Ocean. There's debate about where it should be measured from and to, but it's at least 3,900 mi (6,200km) long.

3. The mouth of the Amazon, where it flows into the Atlantic, is 200 mi (322km) wide.

4. There are no bridges across the Amazon—it's either too wide, or in the middle of the rain forest.

5. Every second, the Amazon pours more than 52,000,000 gallons (200,000m²) of water into the Atlantic Ocean.

6. There are more species of fishes in the Amazon than in any other body of water in the world.

8 BIGGEST World Religions

Billions of people around the world follow a religion. These are some of the most popular religions, but there are many more.

1. CHRISTIANITY
2. ISLAM
3. HINDUISM
4. BUDDHISM
5. TAOISM
6. SHINTO
7. JUDAISM
8. SIKHISM

6 Horrible Jobs
of the PAST and
Present

1. Royal Farter
Like a court jester, but with extra wind power. In the 12th century, Henry II of England rewarded his royal farter, called Roland le Pettour, with a grand estate for his years of entertainment.

2. Hazmat Diver
Divers have to dive into dangerous chemicals or sewers. They wear protective clothing and are vaccinated against many horrible diseases.

3. Groom of the Stool
It used to be someone's job to help the British reigning monarch go to the toilet. It was an honor and a position of trust, so only high-ranking courtiers got the job.

4. Odor Judger
People are paid to judge how effective deodorants are by sniffing armpits. There are also odor judgers for mouthwash and toothpaste.

5. Smeller
People sniff broken eggs used in processed foods to make sure they haven't gone stale.

6. Gong Farmer
In the Middle Ages, a gong farmer was paid to remove human waste from toilet pits.

5 Crazy Cures
From LONG AGO

Don't try these at home...

1. For toothache, apply a dead mouse to the tooth. (Ancient Egypt)

2. For stomach ache, catch a beetle and throw it over your left shoulder. (Saxon)

3. To cure warts, rub a piece of meat onto the wart then bury the meat. (Saxon)

4. To cure blindness, grind and mix a pig's eye, red ocher, honey, and antimony (a type of metal) and pour it into the ear of the blind person. (Ancient Egypt)

5. For toothache, catch a frog at full moon, spit into its mouth, then tell the frog to go away and take the toothache with it. (Ancient Rome)

3 Unlucky Deaths

1. Aeschylus, the Ancient Greek dramatist, was killed when an eagle dropped a tortoise on his head.

2. King Bela of Hungary died in 1063 when his throne collapsed.

3. In the 1500s, Hans Steininger was famous for his beard, which was 4.6 ft (1.4m) long. He died when he tripped over it while running away from a fire.

8 Facts About Camels

1. The only wild camels in the world live in Australia. They were imported into the country from the Middle East in the 1800s and decided to stay.

2. A Bactrian, or Asian, camel has two humps. A dromedary, or Arabian, camel has just one.

3. A camel's humps store fat, not water. By keeping most of their fat in one place, camels can keep cooler. Camels with droopy humps are most likely hungry camels.

4. Camels spit regurgitated, undigested food when they're angry.

5. Camels have long eyelashes to keep out the desert sand and three eyelids to wipe it away. They can close their nostrils to keep the sand out, too.

6. Camels don't sweat or pant. The moisture in their breath trickles down a groove below the nose and goes back into the camel's mouth, so they're constantly recycling water.

7. A camel's poop is very dry, so the animal doesn't lose much moisture. People often use camel dung as fuel —it's ready to burn right away.

8. A camel's special adaptations mean that it can travel 100 mi (160km) without water.

6 Unusual Foods

1. MAGGOT CHEESE–sheep's milk cheese that's been left outside in the sun. Flies lay their eggs in the cheese, and when the maggots hatch the cheese is ready to eat.

2. HAKARL–a Greenland shark is buried in gravel for a few months, then hung up to dry for several months more. Then it's chopped up and served.

3. BIRD'S NEST SOUP– a soup made from the nests of swifts– birds that build their nests from their own saliva.

4. TUNA EYEBALLS–can be eaten raw or cooked.

5. STINKHEADS–salmon heads are buried in pits and left to rot for a while, then eaten as a fishy delicacy.

6. CENTURY EGGS–eggs ferment inside a clay mixture for several months. The yolk becomes dark green or gray and the egg white becomes dark brown and transparent.

4 ANTARCTIC **FACTS**

1. Antarctica is a continent covered in ice at the Earth's South Pole. Some of the ice rests on land, and some of it extends over the sea.

2. The coldest temperature ever recorded on Earth was -129°F (-89.2°C), taken at Vostok Station in Antarctica.

3. **No one lives on Antarctica permanently, but around 4,000 people stay at research stations there in summer, and around 1,000 in winter.**

4. The largest land animal native to Antarctica is a wingless midge just $\frac{1}{2}$ in (1.3cm) long. Other Antarctic animals, such as penguins, are considered to be sea animals (there are also a few freshwater animals).

4 Arctic Facts

1. **The Arctic is the area surrounding the North Pole, including the Arctic Ocean and parts of Russia, Canada, the US, Greenland, Finland, Norway, Sweden, and Iceland. There's no land at the North Pole, just frozen sea.**

2. The coldest temperature recorded in the Arctic was -90°F (-68°C), recorded in Siberia, Russia.

3. **Four million people live in the Arctic, despite the freezing conditions.**

4. The largest land animal in the Arctic is the polar bear, which is also the largest meat-eating land animal on Earth.

4 *Amazing* Animal Migrations

1. Monarch butterfly–it takes monarchs six months to travel nearly 3,000 mi (4,800km) across North America but they only live for two months, so it takes several generations to make the journey. Somehow, each generation knows where to go.

2. Bar-tailed godwit–flies 6,835 mi (11,000km) from New Zealand to Alaska without stopping to eat or sleep. It's the animal with the longest nonstop migration in the world.

3. Arctic Tern–these birds have the longest migration of all animals, although they stop a few times on their 43,500-mi (70,000-km) journey from pole to pole.

4. Globe-skimmer dragonfly–the longest insect migration, 11,000 mi (17,700km), following the monsoon around the Indian Ocean.

Belize
(Belmopan)

Guatemala
(Guatemala City)

Honduras
(Tegucigalpa)

El Salvador
(San Salvador)

Nicaragua
(Managua)

Costa Rica
(San José)

Panama
(Panama City)

THE **7** Countries
in *Central America*
(and their Capitals)

8 ANIMALS That Should be SMALL But AREN'T

We expect a giraffe or an elephant to be enormous, but the size of these creatures is a bit of a surprise.

1. Lion's mane jellyfish
These huge jellyfish can measure 100 ft (30m) long, and 7 ft (2.2m) across.

2. Japanese spider crab
With a leg span of 12 ft (3.8m) and a maximum weight of 42 lb (19kg), these are an awful lot bigger than your average crab.

3. Green anaconda
This snake can measure up to 30 ft (9m) long and weigh 500 lb (230g).

4. Little Barrier Giant Weta
Giant wetas are the world's heaviest insects, at 2.5 oz (70g). They can have a leg span of 8 in (20cm).

5. Goliath beetle
The world's heaviest flying insect is 4 $^3/_4$ in (12cm) long, weighs 2 oz (60g), and has a 10-in (25-cm) wingspan.

6. Chinese giant salamander
Most salamanders are only a few inches long, but this one is 6 ft (1.8m) long and weighs 110 lb (50kg)!

7. Capybara
Capybaras are the biggest rodents on Earth, weighing up to 145 lb (66kg).

8. Giant fruit bat
These are the world's largest bats, also known as flying foxes. They have a maximum wingspan of nearly 6 ft (1.8m).

4 Space Telescopes

These telescopes, and lots more like them, are in orbit around Earth, sending us information about the universe.

1. Hubble Space Telescope
Launched in 1990, Hubble can capture photographs with ten times the detail of ground-based telescopes and has taken breathtaking pictures of the universe.

2. Spitzer Space Telescope
Like Hubble, Spitzer also orbits Earth, but it takes images using infrared light instead of visible light.

3. Fermi Gamma-Ray Space Telescope
This telescope collects and measures gamma-rays generated by supernovae, black holes, and pulsars. It was launched in 2008.

4. Hard X-ray Modulation Telescope
Some objects in space generate X-rays, such as black holes and galaxy clusters—and X-ray telescopes like this one, launched in 2017, are on the lookout for them.

5 Tallest *Ferris* WHEELS

1. High Roller, Las Vegas, Nevada, US—551 ft (168m) tall

2. Singapore Flyer, Singapore —541 ft (165m) tall

3. Star of Nanching, China—525 ft (160m) tall

4. London Eye, UK—443 ft (135m) tall

5. Bay glory, China—404 ft (123m) tall

7 Deep Dark Caves

. . . .

1. Krubera Cave, Georgia, 7,208 ft (2,197m) deep
The deepest cave in the world.

2. Sarma Cave, Georgia, 6,004 ft (1,830m) deep

3. Ilyuzia Mezhonnogo-Snezhnaya, Georgia, 5,751 ft (1,753m) deep

4. Lamprechtsofen, Austria, 5,354 ft (1,632m) deep
Treasure was rumored to lurk in this cave, so it was walled up in 1701 to stop treasure hunters. When it was reopened, treasure hunters' skeletons were discovered . . . but no treasure.

5. Gouffre Mirolda, France, 5,335 ft (1,626m) deep

5 Facts About Pharaohs

. . . .

1. As well as being in charge of Ancient Egypt, pharaohs were also high priests of the Ancient Egyptian religion, and were worshipped as gods themselves.

2. Male pharaohs often had several wives, but female pharaohs tended to have only one husband. Pharaohs had special symbols of royalty including a false beard, which even female pharaohs wore.

3. After a pharaoh died, the idea was that he or she would become a god, which was one of the reasons a pharaoh's funeral and tomb were so elaborate.

4. In the Old and Middle Kingdoms, between 2628 and 1638 BCE, pharaohs were buried in pyramids built on the edge of the desert near the Ancient Egyptian capital city, Memphis.

5. In the New Kingdom, between 1504 and 1069 BCE, pharaohs were buried in tombs in the Valley of the Kings near the new capital city of Ancient Egypt, Thebes.

6. Mammoth Cave, Kentucky, US, 360 mi (580km) long
The longest cave we know about.

7. The Sarawak Chamber, Malaysia, chamber 2,000 ft (600m) long, 1,300 ft (400m) wide, and 330 ft (100m) high
The world's biggest underground chamber.

5 EXTREME Marathons

Some people are just too tough to run only a marathon (26.2 mi (42.195km). They're only happy with something much more grueling.

1. A 155-mi (250-km) race called the Spartathlon recreates the original marathon—an Ancient Greek messenger's epic run at the Battle of Marathon, after which he died of exhaustion. The modern race avoids the last bit if possible.

2. The Marathon des Sables is run for 158 mi (254km) in the extreme heat of the Sahara Desert.

3. The Sri Chinmoy Self-Transcendence 3,100 Mile Race is the longest race in the world. It's run around a single block in Queens, New York—5,649 laps—over 52 days.

4. The Barkley Marathon is a 100-mi (160-km) race run in Tennessee over an unmarked course. Only 15 people have finished, although the race has been held for the last 33 years.

5. The 6,633 Arctic Ultra covers 350 mi (563km) of Arctic ice. Only 12 runners begin the race, and most of them don't finish.

11 Haunted Places

Do you believe in ghosts? If so, here are some places it might be best to avoid.

1. Glamis Castle, Angus, Scotland
Ghosts include (among others) King Malcolm II of Scotland, Earl Beardie (who is reported to play cards with the Devil in one of the castle rooms), a Gray Lady, and a butler.

2. Paris catacombs, France
Beneath the streets of Paris lies an enormous underground cemetery. There have been hundreds of ghost sightings.

3. Monte Cristo homestead, New South Wales, Australia
This manor house is haunted by the ghosts of the original owners and their maid.

4. Chillingham Castle, Northumberland, England
Haunted by Lady Mary Berkeley, whispering voices in the library, a woman who steps out of a portrait in the nursery, a white lady in the basement, and a whole funeral procession in the garden.

5. The Whaley House, California, US

The house was built on the site of a gallows and is haunted by one of the people hanged there, as well as members of the Whaley family, and a ghost dog who licks visitors' legs!

6. The Palace of Versailles, France

Many ghosts have been seen here. Most famous is the ghost of Marie Antoinette, Queen of France, who was executed by guillotine in the French Revolution.

7. The B3212 road, Devon, England

This road is supposed to be haunted by a disembodied pair of hairy hands, which appear at vehicle windows or even try to take control of motorcycle handlebars.

8. 14 West 10th Street, New York, US

More than 20 ghosts have been reported, including the writer Mark Twain, who used to live here, a gray cat, and a lady in white. It's known as the House of Death.

9. Poveglia Island, near Venice, Italy

From the late 18th century, the island was a quarantine, and later it was a hospital. Thousands of people are buried here, and the island is supposed to be haunted by many of them.

10. Blickling Hall, Norfolk, England

Haunted by the ghost of Anne Boleyn, beheaded wife of King Henry VIII. She is said to appear in a carriage pulled by four headless horses, driven by a headless coachman. She spends the night wandering around the house, carrying her own head.

11. Qiu Mansion, Shanghai, China

The wealthy Qiu brothers built their grand houses next to one another and kept exotic pets in the gardens. The Qiu brothers disappeared under mysterious circumstances. Since then, ghostly animals have been spotted in the overgrown grounds of the abandoned houses.

5 Facts About Ostriches

1. Ostriches are the biggest birds in the world, up to 9 ft (2.7m) tall and weighing about 350 lb (160kg).

2. One ostrich egg is the equivalent of 24 chicken eggs—that's the biggest egg in the world.

3. An ostrich can sprint along at up to 43 mi (70km) per hour, covering 16 ft (5m) in one stride.

4. Ostriches don't drink—they get all the water they need from the food they eat, which includes plants, insects, and lizards.

5. Ostriches can be dangerous—they have long, sharp claws and have been known to kill lions when attacked. They have also killed people.

4 Tiny Dinosaurs

Not all dinosaurs were massive great stomping monsters. These were all smaller than today's house pets—from a small rabbit to a cocker spaniel.

1. MICRORAPTOR

A dinosaur with long feathers on all four of its limbs, Microraptor could probably glide from tree to tree. It measured up to 30 in (77cm) long and weighed 2 lb (1kg).

2. COMPSOGNATHUS

A fast-running meat-eater, Compsognathus weighed around 7 lb (3kg) and measured 26 in (65cm) from nose to tail.

3. LESOTHOSAURUS

Small and agile, Lesothosaurus had five "fingers" on each front limb. It was around 3 ft (1m) long and weighed up to 22 lb (10kg).

4. BAMBIRAPTOR

A birdlike feathered dinosaur, the cutely named Bambiraptor was about 3 ft (1m) long and probably weighed around 7lb (3kg).

9 Deadly Volcanic Eruptions

These volcanic eruptions are the worst since records began. The worst one of all—the Mount Tambora eruption in 1815—caused famines because the ash from the volcano affected the weather all over the world.

1. **Mount Tambora, Indonesia, 1815**

2. Krakatoa, Indonesia, 1883

3. **Mount Pelée, Martinique, 1902**

4. Nevado del Ruiz, Colombia, 1985

5. **Mount Unzen, Japan, 1792**

6. Mount Vesuvius, Italy, 79 CE

7. **Grimsvötn, Iceland, 1783**

8. Kelud, Indonesia, 1586

9. **Santa Maria, Guatemala, 1902**

4 PREHISTORIC Land Predators

1. Andrewsarchus was a huge and terrifying predatory mammal. It was 20 ft (6m) long and measured up to 7 ft (2m) at the shoulder. It died out 36 million years ago.

2. Smilodon was a saber-toothed cat a bit shorter than an African lion but nearly twice as heavy. It probably lived and hunted in packs like modern lions. It died out around 10,000 years ago.

3. At 48 ft (14.5m) long and 5 ft (1.5m) thick, Titanoboa was the largest snake ever. It lived 60 million years ago.

4. The giant short-faced bear hunted in South America until 11,000 years ago. It measured up to 11.5 ft (3.5m) tall standing upright.

6 FACTS About Volcanoes

1. Volcanoes form when red-hot, molten rock pushes up through the Earth's crust.

2. When molten rock is underground it's known as magma. Above ground, spewed out by a volcano, it's called lava.

3. When a volcano erupts, a pyroclastic flow can shoot out at up to 430 mph (700km/h) and temperatures of up to 1,800°F (1,000°C).

4. Yellowstone National Park, is an enormous volcano. It hasn't erupted for 70,000 years.

5. The area around the edge of the Pacific Ocean is known as the "ring of fire" because it's where plates in the Earth's crust meet, making it prone to volcanoes and earthquakes.

6. There are 452 volcanoes in the ring of fire.

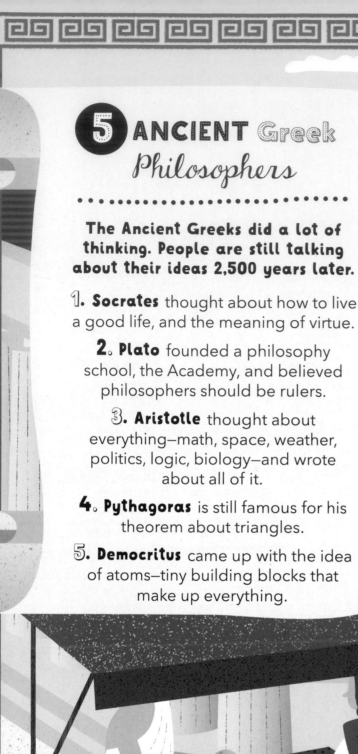

5 ANCIENT Greek Philosophers

The Ancient Greeks did a lot of thinking. People are still talking about their ideas 2,500 years later.

1. **Socrates** thought about how to live a good life, and the meaning of virtue.

2. **Plato** founded a philosophy school, the Academy, and believed philosophers should be rulers.

3. **Aristotle** thought about everything—math, space, weather, politics, logic, biology—and wrote about all of it.

4. **Pythagoras** is still famous for his theorem about triangles.

5. **Democritus** came up with the idea of atoms—tiny building blocks that make up everything.

4 Bloodsucking *Monsters* From Around the World

Fanged vampires that come from Transylvania, turn into bats, and wear swirling capes are just one kind of bloodsucking monster. Here are some others.

1. **Greece:** bloodsuckers come in the form of a half woman, half winged snake.

2. **Malaysia:** the Penanggalan is a bloodsucking flying head.

3. **Australia:** the Yara-ma-yha-who is small, red, and hangs from trees, with suckers on its hands and feet to drain its victims' blood.

4. **China:** vampires have green or pink hair and red eyes.

4 ANIMAL PARTNERSHIPS

Some animals get together to help one another out because it gives them an advantage they wouldn't have otherwise.

1. **African oxpeckers and large animals**
Oxpecker birds eat parasites that live on the skin of animals such as rhinos, zebras, buffalo, and elephants—they get food and the big animals get cleaned.

2. **Clownfish and sea anemones**
Clownfish are immune to the sting of the anemone, so they can stay safe in their stinging tentacles. The anemones benefit because clownfish chase away the butterfly fish that eat anemones.

3. **Cleaner wrasse and bigger fish**
Cleaner wrasse hang out at "cleaning stations," where bigger fish come to have their parasites nibbled away by the wrasse.

4. **Pistol shrimps and goby fish**
Pistol shrimps sometimes share a burrow with gobies. The fish gets a place to live, and the shrimp gets protection from predators because the goby warns when danger is near.

37 Plays by William Shakespeare

THE 7 Ancient Roman Days of the Week

1. **Dies Lunae—Monday**
2. Dies Martis—Tuesday
3. **Dies Mercuris—Wednesday**
4. Dies Iovis—Thursday
5. **Dies Veneris—Friday**
6. Dies Saturni—Saturday
7. **Dies Solis—Sunday**

16 Highest-Earning Films EVER

(as of December 2021)

1. **Avatar, 2009**
(earned more than US $2.8 billion)

2. **Avengers: Endgame, 2019**
(earned more than US $2.79 billion)

3. **Titanic, 1997**
(earned more than US $2.1 billion)

4. **Star Wars: The Force Awakens, 2015**
(earned more than US $2 billion)

5. **Avengers: Infinity War, 2018**
(earned more than US $2 billion)

6. **Jurassic World, 2015**
(earned more than US $1.6 billion)

7. **The Lion King, 2019**
(earned more than US $1.6 billion)

8. **The Avengers, 2012**
(earned more than US $1.5 billion)

9. **Furious 7, 2015**
(earned more than US $1.5 billion)

10. **Frozen II, 2019**
(earned more than US $1.4 billion)

11. **Avengers: Age of Ultron, 2015**
(earned more than US $1.4 billion)

12. **Black Panther, 2018**
(earned more than US $1.3 billion)

13. **Harry Potter and the Deathly Hallows Part 2, 2011**
(earned more than US $1.3 billion)

14. **Star Wars: The Last Jedi, 2017**
(earned more than US $1.3 billion)

15. **Jurassic World: Fallen Kingdom, 2018**
(earned more than US $1.3 billion)

16. **Frozen, 2013**
(earned more than US $1.2 billion)

6
Nobel Prizes

Nobel Prizes have been awarded by the Royal Swedish Academy of Sciences since 1901. They are some of the most prestigious prizes on Earth, and are awarded in these six categories.

1. **Physics**   2. Chemistry
3. **Medicine**   4. Literature   5. **Peace**
6. Economic Sciences

3 of the
Wettest Places
in the World

1. **Puerto Lopez de Micay, Colombia**—average rainfall 507 in (12,890mm) per year.

2. Mawsynram and Cherrapunji, India—average rainfall 467 in (11,870mm) and 464 in (11,780mm) respectively per year.

3. **Mount Waialeale, on the island of Kaua'i, Hawaii**—average rainfall 453 in (11,500mm) per year.

5 Surprising
Ingredients
in *Cosmetics*

1. **Poisonous lead was used in makeup in Ancient Greece and Rome and in Tudor England. Women used it to whiten their skin. Queen Elizabeth I used a mixture of lead and vinegar on her face.**

2. Ambergris is a black substance ejected by sperm whales that is used in some perfumes today.

3. **Pearl essence is found in some modern lipsticks and nail varnishes. It sounds lovely, but it really means fish scales.**

4. Cochineal, a red dye made from crushed beetles, is found in lots of today's cosmetics (and in lots of foods, too).

5. **The Ancient Egyptians used makeup called kohl around their eyes, made from soot, fat, and metal.**

7 Famous NOBEL PRIZE Winners

1. Marie Curie was the first woman to win a Nobel, and one of a very few people to win two Nobels—and in different categories, just to be extra clever.

2. Albert Einstein, the famous physicist with ground-breaking theories about energy and light, won the Nobel Prize for Physics in 1921.

3. Martin Luther King Jr. won the Nobel Peace Prize in 1964 for his work toward ending racial discrimination.

4. Nelson Mandela, civil rights activist and President of South Africa from 1994 to 1999, won the Nobel Peace Prize in 1993.

5. Sir Alexander Fleming discovered penicillin and was awarded the Nobel Prize for Medicine in 1942. He shared the prize with Ernst Chain and Sir Howard Florey.

6. Francis Crick, James Watson, and Maurice Wilkins won the Nobel in Medicine in 1962 for their discovery of the structure of DNA, the chemical that contains all the information that living things need to grow and function.

7. Malala Yousafzai won the Nobel Peace Prize in 2014 for campaigning for the right of all children to an education. She was just 17 when she won the prize.

10 Weird Rainfalls

Reports of animal rainfalls are quite common. They might be caused by strong winds passing over water and sucking up creatures, but no one really knows how these weird rainfalls happen.

1. Sardines: in Yoro, Honduras, there are regular rainfalls of sardines. There's even an annual festival to celebrate them.

2. Tadpoles: in 2009 there were various rains of tadpoles and froglets in different parts of Japan, and one rain of small carp.

3. Frogs: in Odzaci, Serbia, in 2005 and in Rakoczifalva, Hungary, in 2010.

4. Earthworms: in 2011 in Galashiels, Scotland. The rain of worms interrupted a school soccer match.

5. Periwinkles (shellfish): in 1881 in Worcester, England. One of the periwinkle shells had a hermit crab inside it.

6. Fish (spangled perch): in Lajamanu, a desert town in Australia's Northern Territory, in 1974, 2004, and 2010.

7. Worms: in 2007 in Louisiana. Some of the worms fell in clumps and were still alive after they'd landed.

8. Jellyfish: in Bath, England, in 1894.

9. Various sea creatures, including octopus, squid, and starfish: Qingdao, Shandong Province, China, in 2018.

10. Spiders: in 2015 in Goulburn, Australia, spiderwebs containing spiders rained from the sky, in a creepy-crawly migration that occasionally happens in Australia and elsewhere.

49 LANDLOCKED Countries

None of these countries has a coastline. Two of them—Uzbekistan and Liechtenstein—are surrounded by countries that are also landlocked.

1. Afghanistan
2. Andorra
3. Armenia
4. Artsakh
5. Austria
6. Azerbaijan
7. Belarus
8. Bhutan
9. Bolivia
10. Botswana
11. Burkina Faso
12. Burundi
13. Central African Republic
14. Chad
15. Czech Republic
16. Eswatini (formerly Swaziland)
17. Ethiopia
18. Hungary
19. Kazakhstan
20. Kosovo
21. Kyrgyszstan
22. Laos
23. Lesotho
24. Liechtenstein
25. Luxembourg
26. Malawi
27. Mali
28. Moldova
29. Mongolia
30. Nepal
31. Niger
32. North Macedonia
33. Paraguay
34. Rwanda
35. San Marino
36. Serbia
37. Slovakia
38. South Ossetia
39. South Sudan
40. Switzerland
41. Tajikistan
42. Transnistria
43. Turkmenistan
44. Uganda
45. Uzbekistan
46. Vatican City
47. West Bank
48. Zambia
49. Zimbabwe

8 Deadly Snakes

The first four snakes in this list kill more people than any other kind of snake because they're aggressive and live near people. The inland taipan has the strongest venom of any snake, and the king cobra is the longest venomous snake in the world.

1. Saw-scaled viper
2. Indian cobra
3. Common krait
4. Russell's viper
5. Inland taipan
6. King cobra
7. Black mamba
8. Fer-de-lance

5 Very Small Cars

These teeny tiny cars are some of the smallest that have ever been made and sold. They were all manufactured in the 1950s and 1960s, when there was a fashion for micro cars.

1. **Peel P50**
length: 4.5 ft (1.371m)
width: 3.42 ft (1.041m)
height: 3.94 ft (1.2m)

2. **Eshelman Adult Sport Car**
length: 5.25 ft (1.6m)
width: 3 ft (91cm)
height: 2.66 ft (81cm)

3. **The Mivalino**
length: 9.26 ft (2.82m)
width: 4 ft (1.22m)
height 3.67 ft (1.2m)

4. **Heinkel Kabine**
length: 8.37 ft (2.55m)
width: 4.49 ft (1.37m)
height: 4.33 ft (1.32m)

5. **The Isetta**
length: 7.55 ft (2.3m)
width: 4.66 ft (1.42m)
height: 4.33 ft (1.32m)

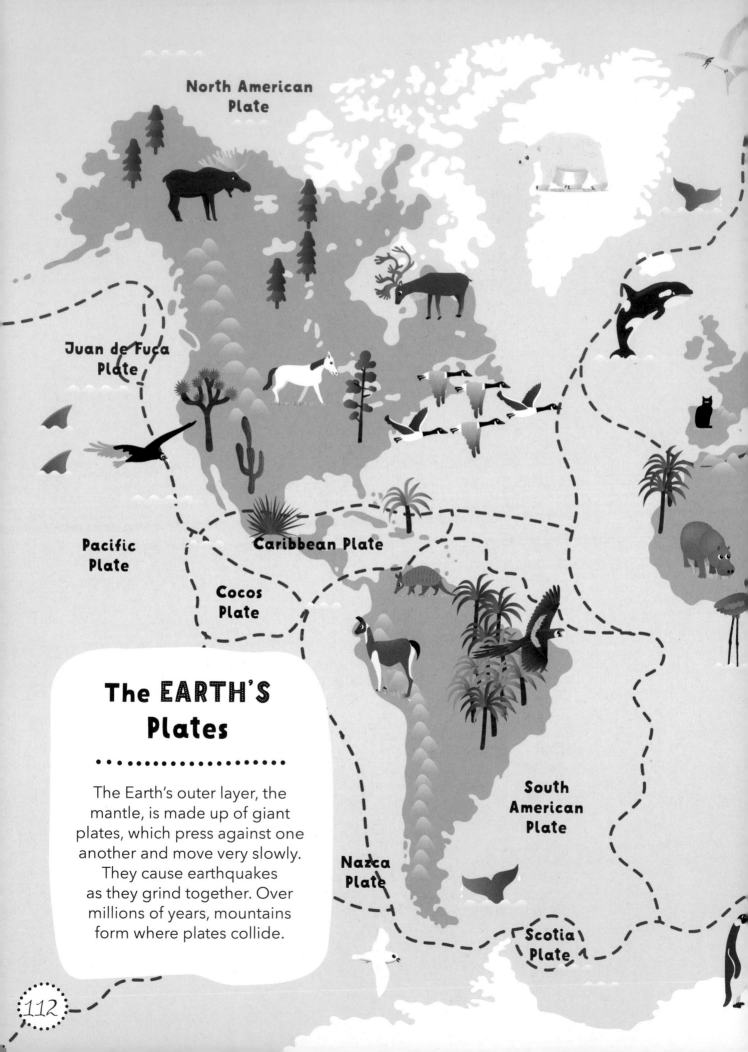

North American
Plate

Juan de Fuca
Plate

Pacific
Plate

Caribbean Plate

Cocos
Plate

The EARTH'S
Plates

· · · · · · · · · · · · · · · · · · · ·

The Earth's outer layer, the
mantle, is made up of giant
plates, which press against one
another and move very slowly.
They cause earthquakes
as they grind together. Over
millions of years, mountains
form where plates collide.

South
American
Plate

Nazca
Plate

Scotia
Plate

Eurasian
Plate

Arabian
Plate

African Plate

Indian
Plate

Philippine
Plate

Pacific
Plate

Indo-
Australian
Plate

Antarctic Plate

113

5 Facts About the Planet Mercury

1. **Mercury is the smallest planet in our solar system—it's about half the size of Earth. It's also the closest planet to the Sun.**

2. Mercury is named after the Ancient Roman messenger god.

3. **It has extremes of temperature: 800°F (430°C) during the day and -270°F (-170°C) at night!**

4. **A day on Mercury lasts 59 Earth days (that's how long it takes Mercury to spin around once on its axis).**

5. A year on Mercury lasts 88 Earth days (that's how long it takes Mercury to orbit the Sun).

5 Animal Extremophiles

Extremophiles are creatures that thrive in extreme conditions—for example, where there's no light, or where it's very hot or cold. Bacteria can live just about anywhere, but we're limiting this list to animals.

1. **The Himalayan jumping spider lives 22,000 ft (6,700m) high in the Himalaya mountain range— higher than almost any other creature. Nothing else lives that high up for it to eat, so the spider relies on finding creatures that have been blown up the mountain by the wind.**

2. Pompeii worms live in hydrothermic vents, which lie deep on the seabed belching out an extremely hot mixture of chemicals. The worms live inside tubes in the vents. No one is sure how they survive temperatures reaching 175°F (80°C).

3. **Sahara desert ants run quickly across superheated Saharan sand, which reaches 160°F (70°C).**

4. Red flat bark beetles can withstand freezing temperatures in the Arctic of -150°F (-100C).

5. **Tardigrades are microscopic animals, also known as water bears, and they are the toughest of the lot. They can survive radiation, extreme pressure, extreme cold and heat, and drought (they can somehow survive without water for years).**

13 Odd-sounding Book Titles

These titles are of books that were actually published. Some of them are still available to buy.

1. **Fancy Coffins to Make Yourself**   2. Eating People is Wrong

3. **Knitting with Dog Hair**   4. What's Your Poo Telling You?

5. **How to Avoid Huge Ships**   6. Outwitting Squirrels   7. **Farming With Dynamite**   8. Talks With Trees: A Plant Psychic's Interviews With Vegetables, Flowers and Trees   9. **Cheese Problems Solved**   10. Zombie Raccoons and Killer Bunnies   11. **What Moles Tell You About Yourself**   12. The Mushroom in Christian Art   13. **History and Social Influence of the Potato**

9 MYTHICAL BEASTS

1. **BASILISK**—weird cross between a snake and a cockerel from European legend. It can kill just by looking at you.

2. **WEREWOLF**—people who change into wolf-human creatures at full moon, in northern European folklore.

3. **BUNYIP**—man-eating swamp monster of Aboriginal Australian mythology.

4. **SPHINX**—a lion's body (sometimes with wings) and a human head, from Ancient Greek and Egyptian mythology.

5. **THE KRAKEN**—huge, many-tentacled sea monster from northern European folklore.

6. **KELPIE**—from Celtic folklore, kelpies are shape-shifters who lure people to a horrible death.

7. **THE MONGOLIAN DEATH WORM**—enormous red worm that lurks in the Gobi Desert, according to Mongolian mythology.

8. **MOKELE MBEMBE**—enormous, dinosaur-like creature that overturns boats in the lakes and rivers of the Congo River Basin in Africa.

9. **THE YETI**—also known as the Abominable Snowman, an apelike creature that is said to live in the Himalayan mountain range.

7 Jokes About DOGS

1. What's the difference between a dog and a marine biologist?

One wags a tail and the other tags a whale.

2. What do a dog and a phone have in common?

They both have collar ID.

3. What do you call a really cold dog?

A pupsicle.

4. What do you get if you cross a sheepdog with a daffodil?

A collie-flower.

5. What's a dog's favorite musical instrument?

A trombone.

6. What do you get if you cross a dog with a calculator?

A friend you can count on.

7. What do you call a dog that does magic tricks?

A Labracadabrador.

11 Coral Reef Creatures

1. The clown triggerfish spurts water at starfish to knock them off the coral, then eats them.

2. Sea snakes breathe air but spend almost all their time in water. They're extremely venomous and could kill a human, but rarely bite.

3. The purple dottyback is a fish that can change color to blend in with its surroundings.

4. Sea slugs are very brightly colored to warn predators that they aren't good to eat.

5. The moray eel has an extra set of jaws near the back of its throat to make sure its prey can't get away.

6. The parrotfish eats the soft living parts of a coral reef, while the rocky parts get passed through its body as sand.

8 ANIMALS THAT USE TOOLS

We used to think that human beings were pretty much the only clever tool users on the planet, but we were wrong. It turns out there are lots!

1. CROWS
Members of the crow family use sticks and feathers to wiggle out food, and to move objects too big to move with their beaks.

2. CHIMPANZEES
Chimps use stones to crack nuts, sponges to soak up water, and sticks to extract termites from their mounds.

3. GORILLAS
Gorillas use sticks as walking sticks, and logs to make bridges across rivers.

4. ORANGUTANS
Orangutans use sticks to probe logs for honey.

5. DOLPHINS
Bottlenose dolphins use sponges to unearth their prey without hurting their snouts.

6. OCTOPUSES
Octopuses use coconut shells as armor against predators. They even carry the shells to use later.

7. MACAQUE MONKEYS
Macaque monkeys sometimes use human hair as dental floss!

8. SEA OTTERS
Sea otters use stones to hammer shells off rocks and open them.

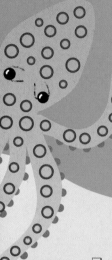

7. A giant clam can live for a hundred years.

8. Brain corals can live for 900 years and grow to be 7 ft (2m) in height.

9. Seahorses are unusual because the male seahorse, rather than the female, carries the eggs around in its pouch before they hatch.

10. A hermit crab uses the abandoned shells of other animals—when it outgrows a shell it has to find a bigger home.

11. Different kinds of reef sharks live on and around coral reefs, including whitetip, blacktip, gray, and Caribbean reef sharks.

5 LAYERS of the ATMOSPHERE

Our atmosphere is a layer of gases that protects the Earth from radiation and keeps us within a fairly comfortable range of temperatures. Thank goodness for that. It can be divided into layers.

1. **TROPOSPHERE:** this is where we live and the weather happens. This layer contains three-quarters of the air and almost all of the water vapor.

2. **STRATOSPHERE**: between around 7 and 31 mi (11km and 50km) up is the stratosphere, where jet engines fly. The ozone layer in the stratosphere protects the Earth from the Sun's ultraviolet radiation.

3. **MESOSPHERE:** from around 31 (50km) to 54 mi (87km), the mesosphere can get really cold—minus 130°F (-90°C).

4. **THERMOSPHERE**: the International Space Station orbits the Earth in this layer of the atmosphere, which continues up to around 300 mi (500km).

5. **EXOSPHERE:** the final layer is very thin. It contains atoms of oxygen and hydrogen, which escape into space.

24

Children's Books by ROALD DAHL

Roald Dahl wrote books for adults as well as children, and he also wrote screenplays for movies. These are his books for children, including two books that are about his own life, *Boy* and *Going Solo*.

JAMES AND THE GIANT PEACH (1961)

Charlie and the Chocolate Factory (1964)

The Magic Finger (1966)

FANTASTIC MR. FOX (1968)

Charlie and the Great Glass Elevator (1972)

Danny, the Champion of the World (1975)

6 PREHISTORIC SHARKS

These sharks all died out long ago, but two sharks still exist today from prehistoric times—the frilled shark and the goblin shark.

1. **Cladoselache is one of the earliest sharks. It was 6 ft (1.8m) long and lived around 400 million years ago.**

2. Helicoprion lived 290 million years ago. It was 23 ft (7m) long, and, oddly, its teeth were arranged in a spiral shape in its lower jaw.

3. **Hybodus measured 6.6 ft (2m) long and lived 180 million years ago.**

4. Cretoxyrhina was 18 ft (5.5m) long and hunted the seas 100 million years ago.

5. **Otodus, which lived 55 million years ago, was huge at 43 ft (13m) long. It is thought to be a distant relative of the great white shark.**

6. Megalodon was, as far as we know, the biggest shark ever. It was up to 52 ft (16m) long and lived until two million years ago.

The Wonderful Story of Henry Sugar and Six More (1977)

THE ENORMOUS CROCODILE (1978)

MY UNCLE OSWALD (1979)

The Twits (1980)

George's Marvelous Medicine (1981)

Revolting Rhymes (1982)

The BFG (1982)

Dirty Beasts (1983)

THE WITCHES (1983)

Boy: Tales of Childhood (1984)

The GIRAFFE and the PELLY and ME (1985)

GOING SOLO (1986)

Matilda (1988)

RHYME STEW (1989)

ESIO TROT (1990)

The Vicar of Nibbleswicke (1991)

The Minpins (1991)

MY YEAR (1991)

7 Facts About Dinosaurs

1. Dinosaurs were reptiles that lived on land. They all shared a number of features—for example, they had straight back legs underneath their bodies, not bent and splayed out like a crocodile's legs.

2. Dinosaurs came in a variety of shapes and sizes—from little dinosaurs the size of a chicken to massive great plant-eating monsters that weighed more than 65 tons.

3. The first dinosaurs appeared during the Triassic Period, around 245 million years ago.

4. All dinosaurs laid eggs.

5. The dinosaurs lived on Earth until 66 million years ago, when a mountain-sized asteroid crashed into the Earth. The impact caused tsunamis and earthquakes, and dust and debris blocked out the Sun's rays. Eighty percent of life was wiped out.

6. The dinosaurs have relatives that still live on Earth today—birds.

7. At the time of the dinosaurs, flying reptiles called pterosaurs swooped across prehistoric skies.

4 Prehistoric SEA CREATURES

These creatures swam in the sea while dinosaurs roamed the land.

1. Elasmosaurus measured up to 49 ft (15m) long—most of that length was its neck!

2. Archelon was a two-ton sea turtle.

3. Tylosaurus looked like a giant snake with snapping jaws, and could grow to 49 ft (15m) long.

4. Liopleurodon might have been as long as 82 ft (25m). It had four huge flippers and a head like a crocodile's.

24 Chinese Dynasties

Ruling families—dynasties—presided over China for thousands of years. The first dynasty, the Xia, was in power for nearly 500 years, from 2070 BCE. The last dynasty, the Qing, ended when the Republic of China began in 1912.

1. Xia
2. Shang
3. Western Zhou
4. Eastern Zhou
5. Qin
6. Western Han
7. Xin
8. Eastern Han
9. Three Kingdoms
10. Western Jin
11. Eastern Jin
12. Southern and Northern
13. Sui
14. Tang
15. Five Dynasties and Ten Kingdoms
16. Northern Song
17. Southern Song
18. Liao
19. Jin
20. Western Xia
21. Western Liao
22. Yuan
23. Ming
24. Qing

6 ANCIENT EGYPTIAN GODS and GODDESSES

· · · · · · · · · · · · · · · · · ·

The Ancient Egyptians worshipped more than 2,000 gods and goddesses. Here is a small selection.

1. **RE: Falcon-headed god of the Sun.** Sometimes also represented as the Sun or a scarab beetle.

2. **OSIRIS: God and chief judge of the Underworld,** represented as a mummified pharaoh.

3. **SETH: God of violence and thunderstorms,** represented by a strange animal with a long snout.

4. **ISIS: Goddess of motherhood and children,** mourner of the dead, and protector of coffins.

5. **ANUBIS: Jackal-headed god of embalmers** who guided the dead through the underworld.

6. **BASTET: Cat-headed goddess of cats** (the Egyptians were fond of cats).

Highest Mountains
ON EACH of the 7 CONTINENTS

· · · · · · · · · · · · · · · ·

1. **Asia (China and Nepal)**
Mount Everest, 29,028 ft (8,848m)

2. **South America (Argentina)**
Aconcagua, 22,835 ft (6.960m)

3. **North America (US)**
Denali, 20,322 ft (6,194m)

4. **Africa (Tanzania)**
Mount Kilimanjaro, 19,341 ft (5,895m)

5. **Europe (Russia)**
Mount Elbrus, 18,510 ft (5,642m)

6. **Antarctica**
Vinson Massif, 16,066 ft (4,897m)

7. **Australia**
Mount Kosciuszko, 7,310 ft (2,228m)

7 Harry Potter BOOKS

The first Harry Potter book, by J. K. Rowling, was published in the UK in 1997. Since then, the books have sold all over the world in the millions, and they've been made into mega-successful films.

1. **Harry Potter and the Sorcerer's Stone (1997)**

2. Harry Potter and the Chamber of Secrets (1998)

3. **Harry Potter and the Prisoner of Azkaban (1999)**

4. Harry Potter and the Goblet of Fire (2000)

5. **Harry Potter and the Order of the Phoenix (2003)**

6. Harry Potter and the Half-Blood Prince (2005)

7. **Harry Potter and the Deathly Hallows (2007)**

15 Space Firsts

1. **First animals in space (fruit flies): 1947**

2. First artificial satellite (Sputnik 1): 1957

3. **First animal in orbit (a dog called Laika): 1957**

4. First human in space (Yuri Gagarin): 1961

5. **First woman in space (Valentina Tereshkova): 1963**

6. First spacewalk (Alexei Leonov): 1965

7. **First spacecraft to land on another planet (Venera 3 landed on Venus): 1966**

8. First spacecraft to land on the Moon (Luna 9): 1966

9. **First person to walk on the Moon (Neil Armstrong): 1969**

10. First space station (Salyut 1): 1971

11. **First spacecraft to pass through asteroid belt (Pioneer 10): 1973**

12. First internationally crewed space mission (Apollo-Soyuz, US/Soviet): 1975

13. **First reusable spacecraft (Space Shuttle): 1981**

14. First spacecraft to leave our solar system (Pioneer 10): 1983

15. **First space telescope (Hubble Space Telescope): 1990**

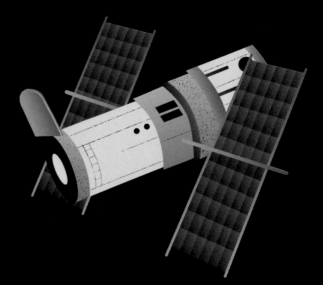

How to Say "Happy Birthday" in 10 Different LANGUAGES

1. Spanish
Feliz Cumpleaños

2. French
Bon Anniversaire

3. German
Alles Gute zum Geburtstag

4. Portuguese
Feliz Aniversário

5. Norwegian
Gratulerer Med Dagen

6. Danish
Tillykke Med Fødselsdagen

7. Swedish
Grattis Pa Födelsedagen

8. Tagalog
Maligayang Kaarawan

9. Swahili
Furaha ya Kuzaliwa

10. Italian
Buon Compleanno

---

6 Extreme Earthquakes

The huge plates that make up the Earth's crust push against one another and sometimes cause earthquakes. They're measured on the Richter scale—earthquakes with a score of four or below aren't very destructive; the biggest one ever recorded measured 9.5.

1. The strongest earthquake ever recorded was in Valdivia, Chile, in 1960—9.5 on the Richter scale

2. Prince William Sound, Alaska, 1964—9.2 on the Richter scale

3. Sumatra, Indonesia, 2004—9.1 on the Richter scale

4. Sendai, Japan, 2011—9.0 on the Richter scale

5. Kamchatka, Russia, 1952—9.0 on the Richter scale

6. Bio Bio, Chile, 2010—8.8 on the Richter scale

6 Amazing Ancient GREEKS

1. ERATOSTHENES measured the Earth using just a stick and the angle of the midday Sun. Because he knew the Earth is a sphere, he could figure it out using geometry, and his answer was almost exactly right.

2. ALEXANDER THE GREAT was a conquering king who defeated the Persian Empire and created his own, which stretched all the way to India—all by the time of his death at the age of 33.

3. HIPPOCRATES was one of the first doctors in Ancient Greece to realize that disease has a natural cause, not a supernatural one. More than 2,500 years after his death, doctors still swear an oath named after him—the Hippocratic Oath.

4. SOCRATES was a philosopher who always said and did what he thought was right. He was sentenced to death for disrespecting the gods and leading young people astray. Although he could easily have escaped, abiding by the laws of Athens was more important to him, and he willingly drank the poison that killed him.

5. ARCHIMEDES was a mathematician and inventor who came up with some of the laws about flotation and volume that we use today. He also invented war machines against the invading Romans.

6. ARISTOTLE was a philosopher who studied the natural world. Some of the scientific books he wrote are still being read today, more than 2,000 years later.

3 AMAZING Ancient Romans

1. Julius Caesar was a politician, leader, and general who conquered new lands and expanded Rome's empire. He tried to take control of the empire, but went a bit too far and was stabbed to death by 23 of his fellow politicians.

2. Augustus Caesar was Julius Caesar's nephew and became Rome's first emperor. After him came a long line of emperors.

3. Spartacus was a Roman slave who fought as a gladiator. He escaped from slavery and led a slave army that nearly overcame the mighty Roman army—but he was stopped and killed in the end.

13 Types of Butterflies

There are thousands of different species of these lovely creatures, found all over the world except in Antarctica. Here are some of them.

1. **Zebra Swallowtail (eastern North America)**

2. Red Admiral (Asia, Europe and North America)

3. **Monarch (the Americas and the Caribbean)**

4. Julia (South America)

5. **Peacock (Europe and Asia)**

6. Queen Alexandra Birdwing (Papua New Guinea) The world's biggest butterfly at 12 in (30cm).

7. **Glasswing (Mexico and Central America)**

8. Peacock Pansy (South Asia)

9. **Viceroy (North America)**

10. Purple Emperor (England)

11. **Tiger Swallowtail (North America)**

12. Blue Morpho (South America)

13. **Montezuma's Cattleheart (Mexico and Costa Rica)**

14 TIMES TO Biodegrade

Different materials take different amounts of time to rot away—and some things take a really, really long time.

1. **FRUIT AND VEGETABLES 5 days–6 months**

2. Paper 2–5 months

3. **CARDBOARD 2–5 months**

4. Cotton T-shirt 6 months

5. **PLYWOOD 3 years**

6. Waxed milk cartons 5 years

7. **LEATHER SHOES 25–45 years**

8. Nylon 30–40 years

9. **ALUMINUM CANS up to 200 years**

10. Disposable diapers 250 years +

11. **PLASTIC BOTTLES 450 years +**

12. Plastic bags 10–500 years + depending on type of plastic

13. **STYROFOAM CUP 500 years +**

14. Glass bottles Never biodegrade

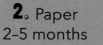

12 SYSTEMS of the Human Body

These human body systems carry out essential functions we couldn't live without.

1. **Circulatory System: moves blood containing nutrients and oxygen around the body.**

2. Respiratory System: allows us to breathe.

3. **Endocrine System: produces chemicals that control things like growth.**

4. Immune System: defends the body against germs and disease.

5. **Digestive System: breaks down food and absorbs the nutrients.**

6. Lymphatic System: makes and moves lymph—a fluid containing white blood cells that help the body fight infection.

7. **Reproductive System: allows humans to have babies.**

8. Nervous System: includes the brain, spinal cord, and nerves, and controls all of our actions, both voluntary and involuntary, such as breathing.

9. **Skeletal System: made up of bones, tendons, cartilage, and ligaments, it protects the body's internal organs, gives the body shape and helps it move.**

10. Muscular System: works with the skeletal system to control the body's movements, and also keeps the heart pumping blood.

11. **Urinary System: allows us to get rid of waste products in the form of urine.**

12. Integumentary System: also known as the skin, the body's largest organ.

7 Jokes About Ancient Egyptian Mummies

1. **What did the angry Egyptian mummy do?**

He flipped his lid.

2. Which Egyptian mummy was very large?

Two-ton Khamun.

3. **Why are Egyptian mummies always stressed?**

They're bound to be uptight.

4. Where do Egyptian mummies go for a swim?

The Dead Sea.

5. **Who did the mummy invite to the Ancient Egyptian party?**

Anyone he could dig up.

6. Why can you trust an Egyptian mummy with your secrets?

Because they can keep things under wraps for thousands of years.

7. **What do Egyptian mummies do on their vacations?**

They unwind a little.

7 PROVERBS From AROUND the WORLD

A proverb is a saying that expresses advice or makes a statement about life. "A bird in the hand is worth two in the bush" is an example in English. Ponder the wisdom of these proverbs from around the world.

1. **A flea can trouble a lion more than a lion can trouble a flea. (Kenyan)**

2. If you go to a donkey's house, don't talk about ears. (Jamaican)

3. **In a battle between elephants, the ants get squashed. (Thai)**

4. The most beautiful fig may contain a worm. (Zulu)

5. **A frog in a well does not know the great sea. (Japanese)**

6. Don't insult the alligator until you've crossed the river. (Haitian)

7. **Someone who chases two rabbits at once will catch neither. (German)**

13 Vital VITAMINS

We all need vitamins to stay healthy. Most people can get all the vitamins they need from eating a balanced diet.

1. **Vitamin A helps your immune system. Sources include cheese, milk, eggs, oily fish, and liver.**

The following 8 vitamins are the B vitamins, which help release and store energy from food, form healthy red blood cells, and are good for the nervous system, skin, and eyes. Sources include fruit, vegetables, eggs, meat, fish, and wholegrain bread.

2. Thiamine (B1)

3. **Riboflavin (B2)**

4. Niacin (B3)

5. **Pantothenic Acid**

6. Vitamin B6

7. **Biotin (B7)**

8. Folic acid

9. **Vitamin B12**

10. Vitamin C is good for healthy skin, bones, cells, and blood vessels, and for healing wounds. Sources include fruit and vegetables.

11. **Vitamin D keeps bones, teeth, and muscles healthy. Sources include sunlight, red meat, egg yolks, and oily fish.**

12. Vitamin E is good for healthy skin and eyes and helps the immune system. Sources include plant oils, nuts, seeds, and wheatgerm.

13. **Vitamin K helps blood clot so that wounds heal. Sources include leafy vegetables, vegetable oils, and cereal grains.**

6 Facts About Jaguars

1. Jaguars are big cats found in South and Central America. The biggest weigh up to 265 lb (120kg) and measure nearly 6.8 ft (2m) long.

2. Jaguars get their name from the Native American word *yaguar*, which means "he who kills with one leap."

3. Of all big cats, jaguars are the least likely to attack people.

4. Jaguars eat land animals such as deer, tapirs, and capybaras, and also—because they're good swimmers—fish, turtles, and caimans.

5. Surprisingly, jaguars also eat avocados.

6. A jaguar's jaws deliver the most powerful bite of any big cat—it can bite through the shell of a turtle.

5 DEADLY Bugs

1. **Malaria mosquito**
Its bite injects germs that cause the deadly disease malaria.

2. **Deathstalker scorpion**
Its sting can kill.

3. **Lonomia caterpillar**
Covered in venomous spines that can be fatal if you touch them.

4. **Brazilian wandering spider**
Its bite can be deadly, and the spider is aggressive and can jump.

5. **Africanized honey bees**
Also known as killer bees, they can kill if they attack in a swarm.

13 Ballroom Dances

Dancers enter highly competitive international ballroom dance competitions in these dances. Numbers 1–5 are classified as "standard" or "smooth" ballroom dances, and the rest are called "Latin" dances.

1. **Waltz** 2. Viennese Waltz
3. **Tango** 4. Foxtrot
5. **Quickstep**
6. Samba
7. **Cha-cha** 8. Rhumba
9. **Paso doble** 10. Jive
11. **East Coast Swing**
12. Bolero
13. **Mambo**

42 COUNTRIES WITH A REIGNING MONARCH

These countries all have kings or queens (or both). The "Commonwealth" countries—formerly part of the UK and ruled over by the British monarch—are the first 15 countries in the list.

1. United Kingdom
2. Canada
3. Australia
4. New Zealand
5. Jamaica
6. Bahamas
7. Grenada
8. Papua New Guinea
9. Solomon Islands
10. Tuvalu
11. Saint Lucia
12. Saint Vincent & the Grenadines
13. Antigua and Barbuda
14. Eswatini (formerly Swaziland)
15. Saint Kitts & Nevis
16. Denmark
17. Sweden
18. Norway
19. Liechtenstein
20. Luxembourg
21. Belgium
22. Netherlands
23. Spain
24. Monaco
25. Vatican City
26. Brunei
27. Jordan
28. United Arab Emirates
29. Saudi Arabia
30. Kuwait
31. Qatar
32. Oman
33. Bahrain
34. Morocco
35. Belize
36. Lesotho
37. Japan
38. Cambodia
39. Bhutan
40. Malaysia
41. Thailand
42. Tonga

The 5 FOOD Groups

All foods can be put into one of these groups. To be healthy we need to eat a balanced diet, including foods from all five groups.

1. **Carbohydrates**—including starchy foods such as pasta and rice, grains, potatoes, and bread.

2. Protein—including meat, fish, eggs, nuts, lentils, and tofu.

3. **Dairy products**—including milk, yogurt, and cheese.

4. Fruit and vegetables—we should eat lots of these, fresh, frozen, or canned.

5. **Fats and sugars**—including butter and oil, desserts, and cakes. Don't eat too many of these.

6 Dangerous SPIDERS

Most spiders aren't dangerous at all, but keep away from these venomous creepy-crawlies.

1. Brazilian wandering spider— can travel the world in banana boxes!

2. Brown recluse spider— small but dangerous in the US.

3. Funnel-web spider— Australian spider that can be deadly to people.

4. Black widow spider— highly venomous, found in North and Central America.

5. Brown widow spider— its venom is more powerful than the black widow's, but the spider isn't as aggressive.

6. Redback spider— venomous but not usually aggressive.

3 INCREDIBLE INSECT Facts

1. There are more kinds of insects than any other group of animal. They make up more than three-quarters of all animal species.

2. Beetles are the most common insect. In fact there are more species of beetles than any other living thing on the planet. There are more than 350,000 species that we know about, and no doubt many more waiting to be discovered.

3. It's estimated that there are 200 million insects for every human being on the planet.

9 Facts About the Sun

Without the Sun, planet Earth would be dark, cold, and lifeless. So it's just as well it's there, really. Here are some facts about it.

1. **Our Sun is a star—a giant ball of burning gas—92,957,130 mi (149,597,893km) from Earth.**

2. Light from the Sun takes about eight minutes to reach Earth.

3. **The Sun is made up mostly of hydrogen (75 percent) and helium (23 percent), plus small quantities of other elements.**

4. The Sun is a medium-sized star.

5. **The element helium was discovered in the Sun before it was discovered on Earth, and is named after the Greek word for sun, *helios*.**

6. The outer layer of the Sun is called the corona. It extends millions of miles into space, but we can only see it when the Moon is between the Earth and the Sun—an eclipse.

7. **The temperature of the Sun varies, with cooler sun spots, but its surface is around 10,000°F (5,500°C). The Sun's core is around *27 million*°F (15 million °C)!**

8. In about 5 billion years, the Sun will run out of fuel and expand to become a red giant, engulfing the Earth.

9. **Never look at the Sun directly—you will seriously damage your eyes if you do.**

4 Divisions of the Ancient Roman Army

The Roman Army was the most powerful of its time. It was organized into Legions, with about 30 Legions altogether. Each Legion contained 5,120 men (no women allowed), made up like this:

1. **CENTURIES**—there were 80 legionaries in a century (at first there were 100, hence the name, but the number was reduced).

2. **COHORTS**—there were six centuries in a cohort.

3. **PRIMA COHORS**—there were 10 centuries in one prima cohors.

4. **LEGION**—there were nine cohorts and one prima cohors in a Legion.

7 Historical CURES for BALDNESS

Throughout history, people have gone to surprising lengths to keep a good head of hair. But none of these "cures" made any difference at all.

1. Burn bees, then rub the ash onto the scalp. (Saxon)

2. Mix together fat from a hippo, a crocodile, a tomcat, a snake, and an ibex and apply the mixture to the head. (Ancient Egypt)

3. Put dead mice in a sealed jar, bury it beside a fire, and leave it for a year. Then take it out and rub it onto the head, taking care to wear gloves to prevent hairy fingers. (Ancient Britain)

4. Apply a mixture of horseradish, pigeon droppings, beet, and spices. (Ancient Greece)

5. Rub myrrh berries into the scalp. (Ancient Rome)

6. Apply cold tea and lemon slices. (Victorian Britain)

7. Spend 15 minutes a day underneath a device called the Thermocap that directs heat and blue light onto the scalp. (1920s America)

The 27 Moons of Uranus

The planet Uranus, the seventh farthest away from the Sun in our solar system, has 27 known moons. They're divided into three groups—thirteen inner moons, five major moons, and nine irregular moons. The major moons are Ariel, Miranda, Titania, Oberon, and Umbriel. All 27 are named after characters from the works of William Shakespeare and Alexander Pope. Here they all are in alphabetical order.

1. Ariel
2. Belinda
3. Bianca
4. Caliban
5. Cordelia
6. Cressida
7. Cupid
8. Desdemona
9. Ferdinand
10. Francisco
11. Juliet
12. Mab
13. Margaret
14. Miranda
15. Oberon
16. Ophelia
17. Perdita
18. Portia
19. Prospero
20. Puck
21. Rosalind
22. Setebos
23. Stephano
24. Sycorax
25. Titania
26. Trinculo
27. Umbriel

4 Facts About Pus

Pus is the yellowish sticky stuff that you sometimes see in a nasty wound or spot. What is it, and why is it there?

1. **Pus is a sure sign that a wound or spot is infected.**

2. White blood cells target and kill the causes of infection. Pus is made of dead white blood cells, body tissue, and bacteria.

3. **It can be green or brown as well as yellow, and sometimes it smells bad.**

4. "Pustule" means a pus-filled spot, and "purulent" means "producing pus."

5 Real-life Wilderness SURVIVAL STORIES

1. Juliane Koepcke was 17 in 1971 when her plane crashed in the Amazon rain forest. She was the only survivor. Wearing a mini dress and one sandal, with a broken collar bone and no food apart from a few candies, she managed to survive. She walked for ten days until she found people, and made a full recovery.

3 LARGE LAKES

1. **The Caspian Sea borders Russia, Kazakhstan, Turkmenistan, Azerbaijan, and Iran. It has a volume of 18,800 mi³ (78,200km³) and an area of 144,000 mi² (374,000km²). By volume, it is the largest body of inland water in the world.**

2. Lake Baikal, Russia is the largest freshwater lake by volume, at 5,517 mi³ (22,995km³). It's also the deepest lake in the world, at 5,315 ft (1,620m) deep.

3. Lake Michigan and Lake Huron, two of the Great Lakes in North America, combine to make the largest freshwater lake in the world, with an area of 45,410 mi² (117,612km²), although some people say they are completely separate lakes.

2. Mauro Prosperi was running in a 158-mi (254-km) marathon across the Sahara Desert when he got lost in a sandstorm. He survived for nine days in the blistering heat and cold desert nights before he met a nomad family who helped him to safety.

3. A plane carrying the Uruguayan rugby team crashed in the Andes mountains in 1972. The crash, and the avalanche that followed, left 16 survivors. Two of them finally set off to find help, and found it after a difficult trek. Eventually, after 72 days on the mountain, all the survivors were rescued.

4. Poon Lim was lost at sea after his ship was torpedoed in the Second World War. He survived 133 days on a lifeboat, the world record for lost-at-sea survival, until he was rescued by fishermen.

5. Joe Simpson and Simon Yates were climbing a mountain in Peru when Simpson fell and broke his leg. Yates was forced to cut the rope to save himself during a storm, but, incredibly, both men made it back to safety. Simpson wrote a book about the experience called *Touching the Void.*

13 KNIGHTS
of the ROUND TABLE

· · · · · · · · · · · · · ·

The story goes that legendary British king, King Arthur, made a round table for himself and his knights so that no one sitting around it could claim to be more important than anyone else. Stories about the Knights of the Round Table have been told for centuries. There are different numbers of knights in different stories, but these knights crop up most often.

1. **King Arthur** 2. Sir Lancelot 3. **Sir Gawain**
4. Sir Geraint 5. **Sir Gareth** 6. Sir Geheris
7. **Sir Bedivere** 8. Sir Gallahad
9. **Sir Kay** 10. Sir Bors de Ganis
11. **Sir Lamorak** 12. Sir Tristan
13. **Sir Percivale**

28 Unusual Holiday Days

Why not mark some of these holidays on your calendar?

1. **Dress Up Your Pet Day (January 14)**

2. Appreciate a Dragon Day (January 16)

3. **National Hugging Day (January 21)**

4. National Gorilla Suit Day (January 31, US)

5. **International Polar Bear Day (February 27)**

6. Pi Day (March 14), The irrational number pi starts 3.1415926535. It's celebrated on March 14 because pi is often rounded off to 3.14.

7. **Something-on-a-stick Day (March 28)**

8. World Penguin Day (April 25)

9. **No Pants Day (first Friday in May)**

10. No Socks Day (May 8)

11. **Dance Like a Chicken Day (May 14)**

12. Hug a Cat Day (June 4)

13. **Badger Day (June 17)**

14. Teddy Bears' Picnic Day (July 10)

15. **National Sleepy Head Day (July 27, Finland)**

16. Rollercoaster Day (August 16, US)

17. **National Dog Day (August 26, US)**

18. Nutting Day (for gathering nuts) (September 14, UK)

19. **International Talk Like a Pirate Day (September 19)**

20. International Rabbit Day (September 26)

21. **World Smile Day (first Friday of October)**

22. World Zombie Day (October 7)

23. **Wear Something Gaudy Day (October 17, US)**

24. World Kindness Day (November 13)

25. **World Toilet Day (19 November)**

26. World Hello Day (November 21)

27. **National Samba Day (December 1, Brazil)**

28. Monkey Day (December 14)

12 FACTS About Chimpanzees, Orangutans, and GORILLAS

1. Humans, gorillas, chimpanzees, bonobos, and orangutans are classified as great apes. Gibbons are also apes, but they're classed as lesser apes.

2. Chimpanzees and bonobos are our closest living relatives. Humans shared a common ancestor with them around 7 million years ago—8 percent of our DNA is the same.

3. Like us, chimps are social animals. They often live in groups of more than 100.

4. Chimps eat different kinds of food, including meat. They hunt in groups to track and kill monkeys.

5. Orangutans live in rain forests on the islands of Borneo and Sumatra.

6. For reasons no one knows, some male orangutans grow huge fleshy disks around their faces.

7. Orangutans eat mostly fruit, but they have been spotted killing and eating small primates.

8. Gorillas weigh up to 400 lb (200kg)—they're the biggest of the great apes.

9. There are mountain and lowland gorillas. Mountain gorillas are the biggest.

10. Gorillas eat plants and insects but no meat. They've developed massive jaw muscles to chew all those plants.

11. A group of gorillas always has a silver-back male as the leader. Challenges to the leadership sometimes result in vicious fights, but otherwise gorillas are mostly peaceful.

12. Gorillas, chimpanzees, and orangutans are all endangered, mostly because their forest habitats are being destroyed by people.

5 Lightning-Fast Plans

These jet planes are the fastest ever. Even thinking about these speeds makes you feel a bit queasy.

1. **The X-43: 6,978 mph (11,230km/h)**
2. Boeing X-51 Scramjet: 3,900 mph (6,276km/h)
3. **SR-71 Blackbird: 2,500 mph (4,023km/h)**
4. Lockheed YF-12: 2,275 mph (3,661km/h)
5. **MiG-25 Foxbat: 2,170 mph (3,492km/h)**

12 COUNTRIES with the Longest Coastlines

1. **Canada–164,988 mi (265,523km)**
2. US–82,836 mi (133,312km)
3. **Russia–68,543 mi (110,310km)**
4. Indonesia–59,143 mi (95,181km)
5. **Chile–48,817 mi (78,563km)**
6. Australia–41,340 mi (66,530km)
7. **Norway–33,056 mi (53,199km)**
8. Philippines–21,064 mi (33,900km)
9. **Brazil–20,741 mi (33,379km)**
10. Finland–19,336 mi (31,119km)
11. **China–18,652 mi (30,017km)**
12. Japan–18,032 mi (29,020km)

5 BIGGEST Meteorite Craters on Earth

Every year, hundreds of pieces of space debris hit the Earth, most of them very small. But occasionally a really big one slams into the planet, leaving a massive crater behind it. Scientists think that all of the following great big holes in the ground are meteorite craters—so just think how big the meteorites must have been.

1. **Vredefort, South Africa: 190 mi (300km) diameter**
2. Sudbury, Ontario, Canada: 150 mi (250km) diameter
3. **Chicxulub, Yucatan, Mexico: 100 mi (170km) diameter**
4. Manicougan, Canada: 60 mi (100km) diameter
5. **Popigai, Russia: 60 mi (100km) diameter**

9 Dizzyingly Tall Buildings

These buildings are currently the tallest completed buildings in the world.

1. Burj Khalifa, Dubai, United Arab Emirates: 2,716 ft (828m)

2. Shanghai Tower, Shanghai, China: 2,073 ft (632m)

3. Makkah Royal Clock Tower, Mecca, Saudi Arabia: 1,972 ft (601m)

4. Ping An Finance Centre, Shenzhen, China: 1,965 ft (599.1m)

5. Lotte World Tower, Seoul, South Korea: 1,819 ft (554.5m)

6. One World Trade Center, New York City: 1,776 ft (541.3m)

7. Guangzhou CTF Finance Center, Guangzhou, China: 1,739 ft (530m)

8. Tianjin CTF Finance Center, Tianjin, China: 1,739 ft (530m)

9. CITIC Tower, Beijing, China: 1,732 ft (528 m)

3 Facts About POOP

1. The scientific name for poop is feces, and it's a vital part of how our bodies function. It's what's left from the food we eat after the body has taken the nutrients.

2. Usually, three-quarters of human poop is water.

3. Poop includes bits of vegetables and other foods that the body can't digest (like tomato seeds and corn kernels), dead cells, fats, and dead bacteria. Now wash your hands.

21 Indian Spices

These are some of the spices used in cooking delicious Indian food.

1. Asafetida 2. BLACK PEPPER
3. CARDAMOM 4. Celery seed 5. CILANTRO
6. Cumin 7. Curry leaf 8. Fenugreek
9. Garam masala 10. Garlic 11. GINGER
12. Green chili pepper 13. Mustard seed 14. NIGELLA SEED 15. Poppy seed
16. Red chili pepper
17. Saffron 18. Star anise
19. TAMARIND
20. Turmeric
21. White pepper

6 WORDS for VERY SHORT TIME PERIODS

1. CHRONON
one billionth of a trillionth of a second

2. PICOSECOND
0.000000000001 of a second, or one trillionth of a second

3. NANOSECOND
0.000000001 of a second, or one billionth of a second

4. MICROSECOND
0.000001 of a second, or one millionth of a second

5. MILLISECOND
0.001 of a second, or one thousandth of a second

6. CENTISECOND
0.01 of a second, or one hundredth of a second

10 Explanations for the Northern and Southern Lights

The Northern and Southern Lights are a natural light show that sometimes appears near the North and South Poles, They're caused by charged particles from the Sun reacting with the Earth's magnetic field. In the past, people came up with more colorful explanations.

1. **The goddess of dawn's chariot (Greece)**

2. Fighting dragons (China)

3. **The gods dancing (Australia)**

4. Spirit guides showing the way to the afterlife (North America)

5. **Fires on which warriors cooked their dead enemies (North America)**

6. Carriages on their way to a wedding party (Estonia)

7. **A flock of swans flying too far north (Denmark)**

8. The swishing tail of the firefox running across the snow (Finland)

9. **The reflection of a huge school of herrings (Sweden)**

10. A bridge leading to the afterlife (Sweden, Norway, and Denmark)

5 Human Parasites

These little critters are all uninvited guests on the human body.

1. Scabies mites
These microscopic mites burrow into the skin to lay their eggs, causing a lot of itching and unpleasantness to their human hosts in the process.

2. Bed bugs
Bed bugs don't live on people but come out at night to drink their blood. The creatures spend the day hiding in cracks and crevices.

3. Demodrex mites
These teeny-tiny mites are very common, and might be living on your eyelashes and face without you knowing about it—they're too small to see.

4. Head lice
These creatures live on human heads. They can be very itchy, and they are big enough to see. They can't jump or fly so they spread by head-to-head contact.

5. Body lice
These are similar to head lice but lay their eggs in clothing. They spend the rest of their time drinking blood and making people itch like mad. Some body lice carry the disease typhus.

6 Facts About *Butterflies*

1. Butterflies are flying insects that live on a liquid diet of nectar, fruit juice, sap, and even animal dung.

2. Butterflies' taste sensors are on their feet, so they can tell whether something is tasty just by landing on it.

3. Butterflies drink with their proboscis, which acts like a straw.

7 COLORS of the RAINBOW

Rainbows are really made up of lots of different colors that overlap one another, so many that we can't see all of them. Most people think of them as seven separate colors. You could remember them with the traditional memory aid— Richard Of York Gave Battle In Vain. The colors always appear in the same order in a rainbow.

1. Red 2. Orange 3. Yellow
4. Green 5. Blue
6. Indigo 7. Violet

4. A butterfly's life is in four parts: egg, larva (caterpillar), pupa (protective shell), and adult butterfly.

5. **Most caterpillars eat plants, but some eat insects, spiders, and insect larvae.**

6. Butterflies can't fly in cold weather because they're cold-blooded.

5 FACTS
About RAINBOWS

1. Rainbows appear when it's sunny and water is falling at the same time.

2. Sunlight bounces off water droplets and the light is split into individual wavelengths, which we see as colors.

3. Sometimes "fogbows" can form, when sunlight bounces off water droplets in fog or mist.

4. Light from the moon can also make a rainbow, although this is very rare. It's known as a lunar rainbow or a moonbow.

5. You can create your own rainbow on a sunny day: stand with your back to the Sun and spray a hose so that it cascades in front of you.

6 Absolutely Appalling Smells

Researchers from the University of California, Berkeley, identified these as the worst sources of terrible odors.

1. One of the world's worst smells comes from a flower called Rafflesia arnoldii or Stinking Corpse Lily—it smells that way to attract flies to pollinate it.

2. Lesser anteaters are much smellier than skunks, which are more famous for their terrible stench.

3. The planet Uranus has an atmosphere of hydrogen sulfide, which smells like rotten eggs, so make a note never to visit.

4. Durian fruit smell so bad that they're banned on the Singapore transportation system, but some people like to eat them.

5. Vieux Boulogne cheese smells terrible too but, again, some people like to eat it.

6. It's no surprise that the researchers found one of the world's worst smells to be human poop—specifically, human poop that had been buried in a barrel in Denmark in the Middle Ages, 700 years ago.

6 BLOODTHIRSTY Pirates

1. The two Barbarossa ("red beard") brothers terrorized shipping in the Mediterranean Sea from their base on the North African coast.

2. Captain Kidd was sent to hunt down pirates in the Indian Ocean for the English but turned pirate himself.

3. Blackbeard is one of the most infamous pirates of all. He captured ships off the coast of America in the 1700s until he was captured and killed by the British Navy.

4. Calico Jack was a pirate in the Caribbean until he was executed in 1720.

5. Mary Read disguised herself as a man to live a life of piracy. She joined forces with Calico Jack and Anne Bonny, another female pirate, but was captured at the same time as Calico Jack and died in prison.

6. Madame Cheng attacked ships in the South China Sea in the early 1800s. She lived a long and successful life of crime.

5 *Ancient* Greek Myths

The Ancient Greeks told some of the best stories ever, full of heroes, gods, monsters, and mayhem. Here are a few of the many Ancient Greek myths.

1. Pandora's Box

The god Zeus gives beautiful Pandora to Epimetheus in marriage (without asking Pandora), along with a present in a box marked "do not open." But Pandora can't resist opening it, and when she does all the evils of the world—poverty, misery, disease, and so on—fly out and can never be put back. Luckily, hope flies out of the box too.

2. The 12 Labors of Heracles

Super-strong hero Heracles has to perform 12 seemingly impossible tasks for the King of Tiryns as a punishment.

3. King Midas and the Golden Touch

Granted a wish by the god Dionysus, King Midas wishes for everything he touches to turn to gold. Unfortunately his daughter turns to gold along with everything else. Dionysus takes pity on Midas, who learns not to be so greedy in the future. Midas's daughter comes back to life.

4. Theseus and the Minotaur

Hero Theseus is tasked with killing the Minotaur, a hideous bull-monster that lives in the middle of a fiendish labyrinth. Every year, Athenian children are sent into the labyrinth for the Minotaur to eat, so this is an important job. Theseus kills the Minotaur, escapes from the labyrinth, and marries the princess.

5. Perseus and Medusa

Perseus upsets a king and has to bring him a Gorgon's head as a punishment. Gorgons, hideous snake-haired women, turn people to stone when they look them in the eye. With help from the gods, and a mirror to avoid looking directly at the Gorgon Medusa, Perseus completes his grisly task.

List of 118 Chemical Elements

Chemical elements are the building blocks that make up everything. They are substances that can't be broken down into simpler substances by an ordinary chemical process. There are 118 known elements, 92 of which are natural (not made in a laboratory by people).

1 H Hydrogen								
3 Li Lithium	4 Be Beryllium							
11 Na Sodium	12 Mg Magnesium							
19 K Potassium	20 Ca Calcium	21 Sc Scandium	22 Ti Titanium	23 V Vanadium	24 Cr Chromium	25 Mn Manganese	26 Fe Iron	27 Co Cobalt
37 Rb Rubidium	38 Sr Strontium	39 Y Yttrium	40 Zr Zirconium	41 Nb Niobium	42 Mo Molybdenum	43 Tc Technetium	44 Ru Ruthenium	45 Rh Rhodium
55 Cs Cesium	56 Ba Barium	57-71 Lanthanides (see below)	72 Hf Hafnium	73 Ta Tantalum	74 W Tungsten	75 Re Rhenium	76 Os Osmium	77 Ir Iridium
87 Fr Francium	88 Ra Radium	89-103 Actinides (see below)	104 Rf Rutherfordium	105 Db Dubnium	106 Sg Seaborgium	107 Bh Bohrium	108 Hs Hassium	109 Mt Meitnerium

57 La Lanthanum	58 Ce Cerium	59 Pr Praseodymium	60 Nd Neodymium	61 Pm Promethium	62 Sm Samarium	63 Eu Europium
89 Ac Actinium	90 Th Thorium	91 Pa Protactinium	92 U Uranium	93 Np Neptunium	94 Pu Plutonium	95 Am Americium

3 ENORMOUS Gem Stones

These hefty gems are some of the biggest ever discovered.

1. Bahia Emerald (752 lb / 341kg)— enormous shards of emerald embedded in a single, boulder-sized piece of rock.

2. American Golden Topaz (10 lb / 4.5kg)— the biggest cut yellow topaz in the world.

3. Olympic Australis (7.61 lb / 3.45kg)— the world's biggest opal.

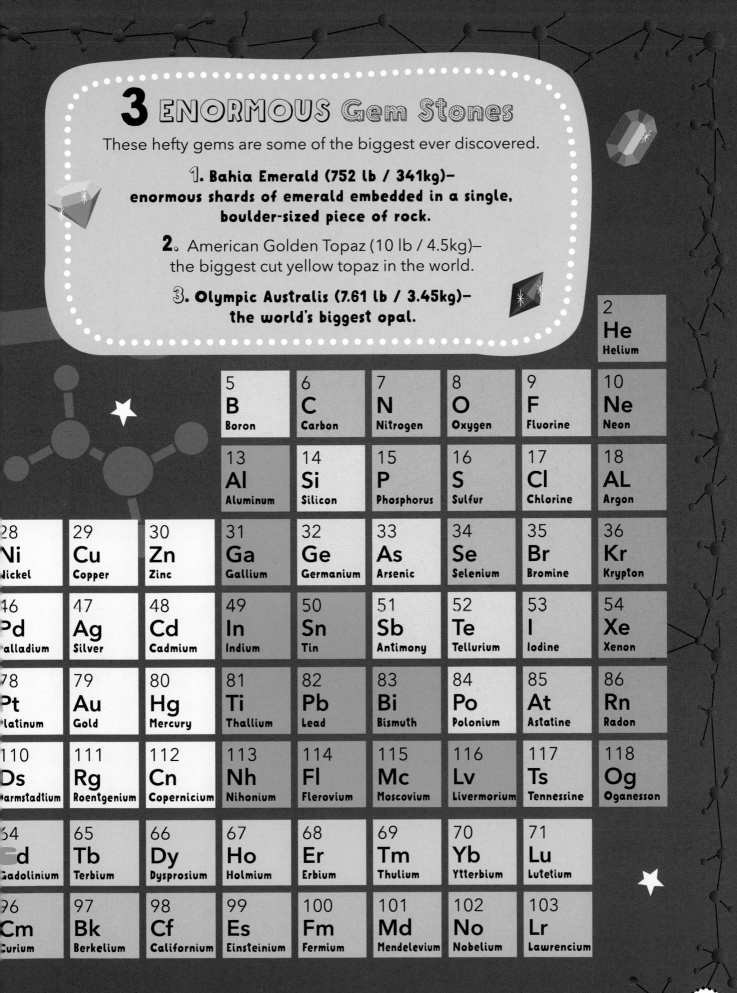

					2 **He** Helium
5 **B** Boron	6 **C** Carbon	7 **N** Nitrogen	8 **O** Oxygen	9 **F** Fluorine	10 **Ne** Neon
13 **Al** Aluminum	14 **Si** Silicon	15 **P** Phosphorus	16 **S** Sulfur	17 **Cl** Chlorine	18 **AL** Argon

28 **Ni** Nickel	29 **Cu** Copper	30 **Zn** Zinc	31 **Ga** Gallium	32 **Ge** Germanium	33 **As** Arsenic	34 **Se** Selenium	35 **Br** Bromine	36 **Kr** Krypton
46 **Pd** Palladium	47 **Ag** Silver	48 **Cd** Cadmium	49 **In** Indium	50 **Sn** Tin	51 **Sb** Antimony	52 **Te** Tellurium	53 **I** Iodine	54 **Xe** Xenon
78 **Pt** Platinum	79 **Au** Gold	80 **Hg** Mercury	81 **Ti** Thallium	82 **Pb** Lead	83 **Bi** Bismuth	84 **Po** Polonium	85 **At** Astatine	86 **Rn** Radon
110 **Ds** Darmstadtium	111 **Rg** Roentgenium	112 **Cn** Copernicium	113 **Nh** Nihonium	114 **Fl** Flerovium	115 **Mc** Moscovium	116 **Lv** Livermorium	117 **Ts** Tennessine	118 **Og** Oganesson

64 **Gd** Gadolinium	65 **Tb** Terbium	66 **Dy** Dysprosium	67 **Ho** Holmium	68 **Er** Erbium	69 **Tm** Thulium	70 **Yb** Ytterbium	71 **Lu** Lutetium
96 **Cm** Curium	97 **Bk** Berkelium	98 **Cf** Californium	99 **Es** Einsteinium	100 **Fm** Fermium	101 **Md** Mendelevium	102 **No** Nobelium	103 **Lr** Lawrencium

11 WOMEN in Space

Since Valentina Tereshkova's pioneering space flight, more than 60 women have traveled to space. Here are a few of them.

1. Valentina Tereshkova of the USSR became the first woman in space in 1963. Her husband was also a cosmonaut, and they had the first baby whose parents have both visited space.

2. Svetlana Savitskaya was the first woman to perform a space walk. She was only the second woman in space, 19 years after Tereshkova.

3. Sally Ride was the first American woman in space in 1983.

4. Helen Sharman became the first British astronaut in 1991.

5. Mae Jemison became the first African American woman in space when she traveled on the Space Shuttle in 1992.

6. Roberta Bondar became the first Canadian woman in space in 1992.

7. Eileen Collins was the first female commander of a Space Shuttle.

8. Yi So-yeon made her first space flight in 2008, when she became the first Korean woman in space.

9. Yelena Kondakova became the first woman to travel on the Russian Soyuz program and on the US Space Shuttle.

10. Yelena Serova became the first Russian woman to visit the International Space Station in 2014.

11. Liu Yang was the first Chinese woman in space in 2012.

5 FACTS ABOUT OUR MOON

1. The distance between the Earth and the Moon varies a bit—on average, it's 238,856 mi (384,401km) away.

2. In relation to the size of the planet it orbits, our Moon is the biggest satellite in the solar system.

3. The temperature on the Moon varies between 243°F (117°C) and -261°F (-163°C).

4. The far side of the Moon is always facing away from Earth. The first time it was seen by people was in 1959, when a Soviet probe sent pictures of it.

5. The Moon is covered with craters left by passing asteroids. The largest is a whopping 1,305 mi (2,100km) wide and 7.5 mi (12km) deep.

6
Round-the-world JOURNEYS

These circumnavigations of the Earth—journeys all the way around the world—were each the first of their kind.

1. First circumnavigation: an expedition led by Ferdinand Magellan was the first to sail all the way around the world. The expedition returned in 1521, but Magellan wasn't on board— he had been killed in the Philippines.

2. First round-the-world solo sailing: Captain Joshua Slocum completed his lonely sailing trip in 1898.

3. First non-stop round-the-world solo sailing: Robin Knox-Johnston completed the trip in 1969.

4. First balloon flight: Brian Jones and Bertrand Piccard made their three-week hot-air balloon journey around the world in 1999.

5. First round-the-world walk: David Kunst made the first confirmed journey, starting in 1970 and ending four years later.

6. First non-stop round-the-world flight: Captain James Gallagher flew a bomber plane on a 94-hour flight around the world in 1949, refueling four times in midair.

20 Plants GROWN For Food

Human beings eat a lot of food— nearly 1 billion tons of vegetables, 2 billion tons of grains, and 564 million tons of fruit, just in one year! These are the crops that produce the most food in the world.

1. **Sugarcane**
2. Corn
3. **Wheat**
4. Rice
5. **Potatoes**
6. Sugar beet
7. **Soybeans**
8. Cassava
9. **Barley**
10. Tomatoes

11. **Sweet potatoes**
12. Watermelons
13. **Bananas**
14. Cabbages
15. **Grapes**
16. Apples
17. **Oranges**
18. Sorghum
19. **Onions**
20. Coconuts

★ FACTS ABOUT THE Vikings ★

1. The Vikings originally came from Norway, Sweden, and Denmark. They began raiding other countries from around 800 CE, sailing across the sea in their longboats.

2. As well as plundering other countries, the Vikings came to stay. They conquered a lot of Britain and Ireland. They were the first people to settle permanently in Iceland and Greenland.

3. Vikings traded all over Europe and into Central Asia—as far as Constantinople (modern-day Istanbul) and Baghdad.

4. Pictures of Vikings often show them wearing helmets with huge horns sticking out on either side, but they didn't really wear helmets like that.

5. Vikings were the first Europeans to sail to the Americas. Vikings led by Leif Erikson landed in what's now Canada in around 1000 CE, and settled for a while, but they abandoned the settlement in the end.

6. "Berserkers" were fierce Viking warriors who went into a trancelike fighting fury during battle. It's where we get our word "berserk."

7. The Normans, who came from northern France and conquered Britain in 1066, were descendants of the Vikings.

5 Birds with BIG Beaks

1. The toco toucan has a beak that measures one-third of its total length.

2. The rhinoceros hornbill has a huge extra feature called a casque on top of its beak, which is bright orange and curves upward like a rhino's horn.

3. Spoonbills have spoon-shaped beaks, which they use to sift food from water.

4. Relative to its size, the sword-billed hummingbird has the longest beak of any bird in the world. It can be longer than the bird's body!

5. Pelicans have beaks with a useful pouch underneath. They use their beaks like nets to scoop fish out of the sea and filter out the water.

5 Incredible BUILDINGS

1. THE COLOSSEUM, Rome, Italy
This huge theater was opened in 80 CE. It could hold 50,000 spectators, who watched games, gladiatorial contests, executions, and plays.

2. STONEHENGE, Wiltshire, England
A circle of huge stones, many of them transported from hundreds of miles away, built in the Bronze Age. No one is sure what it was for.

3. PORCELAIN PAGODA, Nanking, China
Emperor Yung-lo built this 259-ft (79-m) tall, eight-sided structure, covered in glazed tiles. It was destroyed in a rebellion in 1853.

4. THE LEANING TOWER OF PISA, Italy
The foundations of this building, the bell tower of Pisa Cathedral, began to sink soon after building began in 1173. By the time it was finished it leaned sharply, and the tilt has increased ever since. It's 180-ft (55-m) tall and weighs 15,400 tons so it's amazing that it's still standing.

5. THE FORBIDDEN CITY, Beijing, China
This palace complex was the residence of the Chinese imperial families from 1420 to 1912. It contains 980 buildings and is the world's largest imperial palace. It contains the largest and best-preserved medieval wooden buildings in the world. Today, it's a museum.

4 Unusual Hotels

1. **The Palacio de Sal –Salt Palace–is a hotel made entirely from salt in Uyani, Bolivia.**

2. The ice hotel in Jukkasjärvi, Sweden, was the first hotel to be made of ice. Every year, the hotel is remade using ice from a frozen river.

3. **Giraffe Manor, Nairobi, Kenya, is a hotel with a herd of friendly giraffes living in its grounds. They often stick their heads inside the dining room at mealtimes.**

4. At Jules Undersea Lodge in Florida, you have to scuba dive to your hotel room. There's even undersea pizza delivery.

4

Facts About AFRICAN Elephants

1. **African elephants are the world's largest land animals. They measure 11 ft (3m) at the shoulder and weigh around 6 tons on average.**

2. An African elephant's ear can measure 6.5 ft (2m) across, and its footprint can be 1.5 ft (0.5m) across!

3. **An elephant's trunk has more than 40,000 muscles. The trunk is used to smell, pick things up, suck up water, and to touch and cuddle other elephants.**

4. A hundred years ago there were more than three million African elephants. Sadly, today there are only around 415,000.

8 SAYINGS from AROUND the *World*

All languages have sayings that don't literally mean what they say–if someone's pulling your leg, it means they're joking, for example. Why not adopt some of these sayings?

1. Not my circus, not my monkeys
Meaning "not my problem." (Polish)

2. Hanging noodles on your ears
Meaning "joking," rather like "pulling your leg." (Russian)

3. There's no cow on the ice
Meaning "no need to panic." (Swedish)

4. Some days honey, some days onion
Meaning "some days things work out, some they don't." (Arabic)

5. Letting a frog out of your mouth.
Meaning "saying the wrong thing," rather like "putting your foot in it." (Finnish)

6. A raisin in the sausage
Meaning "a nice surprise in something that's already good," like "the cherry on the cake." (Norwegian)

7. Cutting leaves for the dogs
Meaning "wasting time." (Romanian)

8. Having a pig
Meaning "having a piece of luck." (German)

7 Jokes About KNIGHTS

1. When did knights swap places with one another?
During the knight shift.

2. What do you call a knight who likes practical jokes?
Sir Prize.

3. What do you call a knight who likes jousting?
Sir Lance-alot.

4. Where did knights go for dinner?
To the all-knight diner.

5. How do knights find out what's going on?
They watch the knightly news.

6. Where do knights do their training?
At knight school.

7. Why are knights obsessed with their armor?
Because it's riveting.

5 of the LONGEST-LIVING THINGS

• • • • • • • • • • • • • • • •

1. The longest living animal with a backbone is the Greenland shark, which can live for more than 400 years.

2. Nematode worms found in the Arctic ice were thawed out and continued to live and eat. The oldest was more than 40,000 years old—the world's oldest living multicelled animal.

3. Clonal colonies of plants can live for thousands of years too. Pando, a clonal colony of quaking aspen trees in Utah, is thought to be 80,000 years old. It's cheating a bit, because it's the colony that survives and not individual plants, but they're all connected by an underground root system.

4. The oldest living tree that we know about is a Great Basin bristlecone pine in California—it's the oldest tree that isn't part of a colony, at more than 5,060 years old.

5. Glass sponges more than 10,000 years old have been found in the East China Sea and the Southern Ocean.

5 MAD Scientists

• • • • • • • • • • • • • • • •

Some people have gone to extremes in the name of science.

1. Isaac Newton poked sticks into his eye sockets during his experiments on color, and was lucky not to blind himself.

2. During his research into cats' ear mites, Dr. Robert A. Lopez transferred some of the mites into his own ears. Luckily, he didn't suffer any lasting damage.

3. Stubbin Ffirth was convinced that the disease yellow fever isn't contagious but is caused by too much noise, food, and heat. He was so convinced that he tried all sorts of unpleasant ways of getting the disease, including eating a yellow fever patient's vomit. He didn't get the disease, but he was wrong— yellow fever is passed into the bloodstream, usually by the bite of a mosquito.

4. Lazzaro Spollanzani researched how food changed inside the body by eating his own vomit —he ate vomit he'd already vomited up twice before.

5. Hennig Brand discovered the element phosphorus in 1669 after a long and horrible series of experiments, each of which used 50 buckets of human urine.

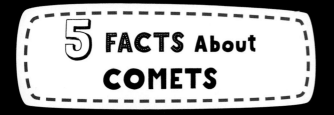

5 FACTS About COMETS

1. Comets are made mainly of frozen gases and pieces of rock and dust.

2. Comets are in orbit around the Sun, so it's possible to predict when we're going to see some of them. Halley's comet, first identified by Edmond Halley, passes close to the Earth every 75 years. The next time it's due is 2061.

3. When Halley's comet was due to pass close to Earth in 1910, the discovery that it contained poisonous gas made people buy gas masks, "anti-comet pills," and "anti-comet umbrellas."

4. When a comet passes close to the Sun, the frozen gases heat up and trail off into space, giving the comet a tail that stretches millions of miles behind it.

5. Comets formed at the same time as our solar system, around 4.6 billion years ago.

How to Say "GOODBYE" in 9 Different Languages

1. Spanish
Adiós

2. French
Au revoir

3. Italian
Arrivederci

4. Swahili
Kwaheri

5. Portuguese
Tchau

6. Hawaiian
Aloha

7. Polish
Do widzenia

8. German
Auf Wiedersehen

9. Hebrew
Shalom

INDEX

Page numbers in **bold** indicate a complete list.